CW01558744

book lovers

thegoodwebguide

book lovers

Susan Osborne

The Good Web Guide Limited • London

First Published in Great Britain in 2003 by The Good Web Guide Limited
65 Bromfelde Road, London SW4 6PP

www.thegoodwebguide.co.uk

Email:feedback@thegoodwebguide.co.uk

Original series concept by Steve Bailey.

10 9 8 7 6 5 4 3 2 1

A catalogue record for this book is available from the British Library.

ISBN 1-903282-42-X

Design by Myriad Creative Ltd

Printed in Italy at LEGO S.p.A.

contents

the good web guides   6

introduction   9

user key   10

1 going shopping   11

2 authors   35

3 publishers' sites and trade news   55

4 literary magazines and newspapers online   68

5 children and young adults   81

6 reading group resources   99

7 literary resources and reference   106

8 literature published on the web   118

9 for writers   123

10 miscellany   132

index   140

the good web guides

The World Wide Web is a vast resource, with millions of sites on every conceivable subject. There are people who have made it their mission to surf the net: cyber-communities have grown, and people have formed relationships and even married on the net.

However, the reality for most people is that they don't have the time or inclination to surf the net for hours on end. Busy people want to use the internet for quick access to information. You don't have to spend hours on the internet looking for answers to your questions and you don't have to be an accomplished net surfer or cyber wizard to get the most out of the web. It can be a quick and useful resource if you are looking for specific information.

The Good Web Guides have been published with this in mind. To give you a head start in your search, our researchers have looked at hundreds of sites and what you will find in the Good Web Guides is a collection of reviews of the best we've found.

The Good Web Guide recommendation is impartial and all the sites have been visited several times. Reviews are focused on the website and what it sets out to do, rather than an endorsement of a company, or their product. A small but beautiful site run by a one-man band may be rated higher than an ambitious but flawed site run by a mighty organisation.

Relevance to the UK-based visitor is also given a high premium: tantalising as it is to read about purchases you can make in California, because of delivery charges, import duties and controls it may not be as useful as a local site.

Our reviewers considered a number of questions when reviewing the sites, such as: How quickly do the sites and individual pages download? Can you move around the site easily and get back to where you started, and do the links work? Is the information up to date and accurate? And is the site pleasing to the eye and easy to read? More importantly, we also asked whether the site has something distinctive to offer, whether it be entertainment, inspiration or pure information. On the basis of the answers to these questions sites are given ratings out of five. As we aim only to include sites that we feel are of serious interest, there are very few low-rated sites.

Bear in mind that the collection of reviews you see here are just a snapshot of the sites at a particular time. The process of choosing and writing about sites is rather like painting the Forth Bridge: as each section appears complete, new sites are launched and others are modified. When you've registered at the Good Web Guide site you can check out the reviews of new sites and updates of existing ones, or even have them emailed to you.

By registering at **www.thegoodwebguide.co.uk** you'll find hot links to all the sites listed, so you can just click and go without needing to type the addresses accurately into your browser.

As this is the first edition of the Good Web Guide Book Lovers, all our sites have been reviewed by the author and research team, but we'd like to know what you think. Contact us via the website or email feedback @thegoodwebguide.co.uk. You are welcome to recommend sites, quibble about the ratings, point out changes and inaccuracies or suggest new features to assess.

You can find us at **www.thegoodwebguide.co.uk**

ACKNOWLEDGEMENTS

Thanks to all who suggested sites for this book, in particular Nick Rennison for a particularly juicy list, and Noel Murphy who generously shared his own research. I would also like to thank all those dedicated and passionate readers whose lovingly tended sites make the internet such an interesting place for book lovers to explore.

On a more personal note I would like to thank all my family and friends who helped me through a very difficult time shortly after I finished writing this book, in particular Mary Upton, whose generous support was invaluable, and my good friend Margaret Jones.

Last, but very far from least, I would like to thank my partner, Hugh, for his unfailing love and support, not too mention his patience.

PICTURE ACKNOWLEDGEMENTS

The publishers are grateful to the following for permission to reproduce their jackets on the front cover:

Kyle Cathie Ltd for **WB Yeats: The Love Poems** edited by Professor AN Jeffares; Penguin Books Ltd for **Sacred Hunger** by Barry Unsworth, illustration by Anne Magill; Harper Collins Ltd for **Duplicate Keys** by Jane Smiley, Random House/Secker and Warburg for **Paddy Clarke Ha Ha Ha** by Roddy Doyle and Random House/Jonathan Cape for **Hotel du Lac** by Anita Brookner.

introduction

If you are a reader and a lover of books you will find plenty to amuse and stimulate your interest in this new addition to The Good Web Guide's library.

Millions of readers go online everyday – there is a wealth of sites to visit. We have chosen some of the best, and our selection is designed to cater for a wide range of literary and bookish interests. Online booksellers, from the well-known to the specialised, book publishers and sites dedicated to favourite authors are all included. We give you details of online literary magazines and newspapers, sites aimed at younger readers as well as those aimed at the growing number of reading groups. This book also provides guidance on sites which provide literary resources, reference and guidance for budding writers.

Don't forget to register the purchase of this book on our web site and if you wish choose to receive online updates for one year.

www.thegoodwebguide.co.uk

user key

£   subscription required

R   registration required

🔒   secure online ordering

UK   United Kingdom

US   United States

going shopping

general booksellers

Although not a bookseller himself, Jeff Bezos, founder of Amazon.com, was quick to see the perfect fit between bookselling and the internet. While many book lovers feel that it's still no substitute for whiling away a weekend afternoon, browsing the shelves of their local bookshop, those living in even the most isolated parts of the world now have a selection of large, well-stocked bookshops at their fingertips. Many of the larger bookselling sites are so rich in articles, reviews, interviews and book excerpts that they can be browsed as if they were glossy literary magazines. Included amongst the reviews below are a couple of US sites which offer the chance to sample some American books that never seem to make it onto UK publishers' lists.

Discounting has become a fixture at most major internet bookshops so we've also included a price checking site to help you to spot the best bargains at the main UK internet bookshops.

amazon.co.uk

amazon.co.uk

Overall rating: ★ ★ ★ ★			
Classification:	Ecommerce	Readability:	★ ★ ★ ★ ★
Updating:	Hourly	Content:	★ ★ ★ ★
Navigation:	★ ★ ★ ★	Speed:	★ ★ ★ ★ ★

UK 🔒

Although its comprehensive review coverage seems to have been cut back a little, amazon's UK arm remains unsurpassed as Britain's best general internet bookshop. The site is packed with information, from author interviews, book excerpts and articles, to hourly-updated bestseller lists. Book recommendations by both staff and customers are a strong feature, although the emphasis tends towards the mainstream rather than the adventurous. Navigation is generally straightforward with plenty of support from the help pages if you do get lost. Category pages all follow the same clear layout so that favourite features are easily found. Free subscriptions to regular email updates on new books in particular subject areas are on offer. New features are often added and are worth bookmarking as they can sometimes be a little hard to track down once they are no longer highlighted on the homepage. Prices are highly competitive, particularly for bestsellers, and buying is both easy and secure. More bargains can be found through amazon marketplace sellers offering new, used or collectable editions.

SPECIAL FEATURES

Reviews amazon's book reviews are its main strength. Major books in each subject area are given a lively broadsheet-length review, sometimes written by experts in the field. Customer participation is actively encouraged and lends a community feel to this corporate site. Customers can accompany their reviews with a star rating from one to five.

Browse Categories Unless you are after a specific title, this is the best path into the mine of information this site has to offer. Each category has its own homepage with some standard features and some particular to that category. These include new and imminent releases, bestsellers, articles, interviews, extracts and editor's choice. Category subdivisions offer the option to narrow down your browsing to specific areas of interest.

Essential Bookshelf This is a particularly useful standard feature which offers reliable recommendations of books for each category, grouped by theme.

Computers and Internet This authoritative and informative page is given a high profile amongst the pushbuttons at the top of the amazon banner. Use the Essential Bookshelf feature on this page to find unpatronising, straightforward articles packed with book recommendations for both the uninitiated and the more technologically savvy.

Listmania A well established feature of amazon.com and growing by leaps and bounds at amazon.co.uk, Listmania consists of reading lists contributed by Amazon customers, complete with their comments about each book.

Lively, accessible and informative, amazon continues to top the UK internet bookseller charts.

www.amazon.com
amazon.com

Overall rating: ★ ★ ★ ★

Classification:	Ecommerce	Readability:	★ ★ ★ ★ ★
Updating:	Hourly	Content:	★ ★ ★ ★ ★
Navigation:	★ ★ ★ ★	Speed:	★ ★ ★ ★ ★

US 🔒

One of the largest book catalogues online coupled with abundant editorial content has made amazon.com's name almost synonymous with internet bookselling. The hourly updated amazon Hot 100 bestseller list, author interviews, book extracts and authoritative reviews plus the offer of free email updates on new publications, will all be familiar to customers of amazon.co.uk. Recommendations are a strong feature based either on browsing habits or information volunteered at registration for the site's Friends and Favourites community area. The vast amount of content available can sometimes seem a little overwhelming but a brief summary of searches and pages recently browsed, displayed at the bottom of the page, should help you find your way back should you get lost. Pages of special interest are worth bookmarking as the browsing history expires after a few days. All items are competitively priced in American dollars and buying is both straightforward and secure.

SPECIAL FEATURES

Friends and Favourites All amazon sites encourage active participation by customers but amazon.com has taken this a step further by effectively setting up an online community.

Free registration allows the creation of a profile describing yourself, together with a list of favourite reviewers and fellow members which amazon gather together into an About You page. Recommendations and reviews based on this information will be added to the page. Other benefits include adding a list of your favourite books to Listmania, an ever-growing database of recommendations, and exchanging views with other members on discussion boards. Friends and Favourites can be reached by clicking on Your Store from the top of the main amazon.com homepage.

Customer Reviews amazon.com give their many prolific customer reviewers a high profile. Many customer reviews are articulate, informed and passionate sometimes eliciting equally passionate ripostes. Details of favourite reviewers together with lists of their reviews can be found by clicking on the See More About Me hyperlink at the top of the review.

The Page You Made This feature offers recommendations based on information gleaned from recent browsing. The page changes as more features and titles are searched and also includes related lists of titles contributed to the Listmania database by members of Friends and Favourites. It can be accessed from the Your Recent History area at the bottom of any page.

Look Inside offers the chance to read sample pages of a wide range of titles available through amazon.com.

The granddaddy of internet bookselling, amazon.com excels in both its range of books and its editorial content.

www.powells.com
Powell's City of Books

Overall rating: ★ ★ ★ ★			
Classification:	Bookshop	**Readability:**	★ ★ ★ ★ ★
Updating:	Daily	**Content:**	★ ★ ★ ★ ★
Navigation:	★ ★ ★ ★	**Speed:**	★ ★ ★ ★ ★

US 🔒

There's a great deal to explore at the website of one of the United States' largest independent bookstores. At this site the emphasis is on the personal, rather than the corporate. Much of the content is presented with flair and a pleasingly idiosyncratic style. Rare, second-hand and new books are all featured with technical and children's books given a high profile. Categories are broken down for easy browsing with the added bonus of the Into the Aisles option on subject homepages, backed up with cross-referencing to relevant sections for selected books. Details of all editions in stock, including rare and second-hand, are displayed alongside reviews. Other features include free registration for a daily book review, an archive of author interviews plus comprehensive lists of literary prize winners.

SPECIAL FEATURES

Staff Picks Calling upon the obvious enthusiasm of its booksellers, Powell's features a large number of witty and informed staff choices. Staff Picks can be browsed by subject or, if you find yourself in tune with a particular bookseller's taste, by employee name.

City Centre Visit this area of the site for the staff pick of the day, opinion pieces and links to a variety of books recommended by Powell's 'section hosts'. Ranging from *Poetry and Writers Magazine* to the American Rivers authority, each section host has a homepage at Powell's which can be reached from the left-hand navigation bar of most screens under the heading Other Voices.

Packed with enthusiastic book recommendations from an American bookseller proud of its independent status, Powell's is a refreshing alternative to corporate internet bookshops.

www.books.com			
Barnes & Noble.com			
Overall rating: ★ ★ ★ ★			
Classification:	Bookshop	**Readability:**	★ ★ ★ ★
Updating:	Daily	**Content:**	★ ★ ★ ★
Navigation:	★ ★ ★ ★ ★	**Speed:**	★ ★ ★ ★ ★
US			

Review coverage at the online home of the largest bookselling chain in the USA, is thorough with lively customer contributions. Click on the pushbuttons at the top of the page for free online courses, bargain books and ebooks, which includes a handy side-by-side comparison of ebook readers. Click Browse Books and scroll down to find out about Special Features, including a section for book clubs and the quarterly Discover Great New Writers roundup.

SPECIAL FEATURES

Barnes and Noble University offers a wide range of free courses, from yoga to classical music, designed to be taken anywhere and anytime, at the student's own pace. Students can communicate with each other and with the course tutor, via a message system.

Meet the Writers has detailed information on a wide range of authors, from Margaret Atwood to Tom Wolfe, including biographical details, anecdotes and a list of similar authors.

A smart, easily navigable site, backed-up by the expertise of the United States' largest bookseller.

www.ottakars.co.uk			
Ottakar's			
Overall rating: ★ ★ ★ ★			
Classification:	Bookshop Info	**Readability:**	★ ★ ★ ★
Updating:	Daily	**Content:**	★ ★ ★ ★
Navigation:	★ ★ ★ ★ ★	**Speed:**	★ ★ ★ ★ ★
UK			

Visitors to Ottakar's website might be puzzled to find that they can't buy books there. Although the site attracts many visitors, apparently very few of them bought books when such a facility existed. Being good businessfolk, Ottakars decided to confine the site's content to book news and a little literary entertainment. Contact details for branches are provided should you wish to order books such as the recommended titles of the month, read and reviewed by Ottakar's staff. Free subscription for a variety of newsletters is offered, including one linked to Outland, the site's regular science fiction, fantasy and horror feature.

SPECIAL FEATURES

Literary Quiz is a weekly multiple choice quiz offering several newly published books as its prize. Regular players can check their progress in the league table.

Yossarian provides an amusing weekly diary of literary gossip. Past issues can be browsed and regular Yossarian updates are available to subscribers.

Books can no longer be bought at Ottakar's website, but it's well worth a visit for entertainment and recommendations.

www.waterstones.co.uk
Waterstone's

Overall rating: ★ ★ ★			
Classification:	Bookshop	**Readability:**	★ ★ ★ ★
Updating:	Daily	**Content:**	★ ★ ★ ★
Navigation:	★ ★ ★ ★ ★	**Speed:**	★ ★ ★ ★ ★

UK 🔒

Run in conjunction with amazon.co.uk, both the layout and the familiar green text may lead visiting amazon customers to assume that this site is simply a duplicate, but Waterstone's have succeeded in putting put their own stamp on it. Magazine style articles include interviews with authors such as Simon Schama, thoughtful author profiles and features devoted to particular genres, which include interesting and knowledgeable and often witty recommendations. Subject homepages each have a monthly Waterstone's Recommends choice. Other features include information on author events in a selection of Waterstone's branches, a Find a Branch facility complete with maps, and a feature length article on the current Book of the Month.

SPECAIL FEATURES

The Jason Cowley Column This monthly column by the *New Statesman's* Literary Editor covers a wide range of literary topics and is both entertaining and knowledgeable.

Waterstone's has firmly stamped its own personality onto this site, run in conjunction with Amazon.co.uk

www.thebookplace.co.uk
The Book Place

★ ★ ★ ★ UK 🔒

As the main online outlet for the Hammicks chain, recently bought by Ottakers, this attractively presented site anchors its content firmly in the bestseller lists. Along with book extracts, interviews and its own monthly features, the site is linked with the lively magazine, *Bookends*. Other features include a thoughtful digest of the Sunday paper book reviews and a direct link to *Publishing News* for book trade gossip.

www.countrybookshop.co.uk
Country Bookshop

★ ★ ★ ★ UK 🔒

This fresh-looking, independent bookselling site, associated with a bookshop in the Peak district, has succeeded in gaining a reputation as a serious rival to some of the more corporate sites. Themed shops for Harry Potter, Tolkien and Buffy the Vampire Slayer offer posters, tee-shirts, DVDs and other related merchandise as well as books. Browsing is straightforward but a quick visit to the help pages will enhance appreciation of this attractive and friendly site.

www.whsmith.co.uk
W H Smith

★★★★ UK 🔒

The emphasis is firmly on bestsellers at W H Smith's straightforward and accessible site. Ebook readers are particularly well catered for with a separate homepage, complete with featured titles, and a wide selection of titles throughout the subject range plus information for those new to ebooks. Click Features to find a small selection of interviews, extracts and magazine style articles or to search the archive for past features. There are links to Smith's Education Zone, a website aimed at both parents and teachers, and to The Internet Bookshop (www.thebookshop.co.uk), a slimmed-down version of this site which includes bargain books on its subject pages. Navigation at this site is both quick and simple.

www.foyles.co.uk
Foyles

★★★★ UK 🔒

Renowned throughout the world as a literary institution, Foyles has become something of a tourist attraction as this simple website acknowledges. Details of Foyles' legendary literary luncheons, of which there have now been over 700, can be found at the site and tickets bought securely online. There are also listings for Foyles' extensive events programme. The site includes several monthly features, often tied-in to publishers' promotions. It also houses The Silver Moon bookshop, now incorporated into Foyles' Charing Cross Road premises, which specialises in women's studies and literature. Each subject, both within the Silver Moon and the main bookshop, has a page of recommendations although editorial content is confined to brief descriptions.

www.thebookpeople.co.uk
The Book People

★★★★ UK 🔒

What you see is pretty much what you get with this bargain basement site. With discounts of up to 75 per cent, the books featured are often hardback editions of titles now available in paperback, although they may be cheaper than the new paperback edition. Orders for books not found on the site cannot be accepted and the help pages emphasise that it operates on a first come first served basis. Worth a visit for the eagle-eyed bargain hunter.

www.dymocks.com.au
Dymocks Booksellers

★★★ AU 🔒

The online bookselling arm of Australia's best-loved bookshop chain, Dymocks should be the first stop for book buyers with a particular interest in Australian literature. The main homepage showcases a range of general titles together with an Author of the Month feature plus a Book of the Month recommended by *The Booklover*, Dymocks's in-house magazine which can be accessed online. Browsing is straightforward and most categories have a sub-section on Australia. Click on Literary Links and Author Interviews for links to many Australian authors' homepages, a set of links to Australian literature sites plus a small selection of author interviews.

shop to buy the book. There are plans to extend the current list of 14 UK shops.

This simple site provides fast, accurate and reliable price comparisons for UK internet book buyers who know what they want.

price checking

www.bookbrain.co.uk			
BookBrain			
Overall rating: ★ ★ ★ ★			
Classification:	Information	**Readability:**	★ ★ ★ ★
Updating:	Weekly	**Content:**	★ ★ ★ ★ ★
Navigation:	★ ★ ★ ★ ★	**Speed:**	★ ★ ★ ★ ★
(UK)			

Streets ahead of any competition in terms of speed and accuracy, BookBrain's site is straightforward, simple to use and will undoubtedly save money for those who regularly buy from UK internet bookshops. The only frills at the site are a selection of featured books and a bestseller list, both of which lead straight into a price comparison for the chosen title. Searches are fast and can be speeded up still more if you can supply an ISBN or publisher for the Advanced Search facility. Don't be put off by the Premier Sponsor banner which heads the list. Just below you will find a further list of prices headed by the cheapest including delivery charges. Click on the direct link to the appropriate

specialist bookshops

Whether it's a computer manual or a script for the local amateur dramatic society, tracking down a book on a particular subject, can sometimes be a bit of a challenge. You'll find a list of bookshop sites in the following pages which offer expert help, advice and information on a wide variety of subjects, from art to travel. Most of the sites listed are the online homes of well-established booksellers with years of experience for you to tap into. Many of them are happy to deal with queries and offer recommendations by email.

The sites in this section have been listed alphabetically by subject.

academic

www.blackwells.co.uk			
Blackwell's Online			
Overall rating: ★ ★ ★ ★ ★			
Classification:	Bookshop	**Readability:**	★ ★ ★ ★
Updating:	Monthly	**Content:**	★ ★ ★ ★ ★
Navigation:	★ ★ ★ ★	**Speed:**	★ ★ ★ ★
UK 🔒			

The Blackwell's bookselling chain is probably best known for its Oxford shop, established in 1879. The homepage of this site represents a gateway into the vast array of books available at Blackwell's. General interests are well catered for in the Fiction, Leisure, Biography and Children's sections but the major areas of expertise are undoubtedly in the more academic and professional departments. Clicking on one of these leads to a subject-related homepage featuring well-chosen selections of new books. Online access is also offered to Blackwell's extensive catalogues through the Browse by Category facility while rare book catalogues can be reached from the Other Blackwell's Products link at the bottom of the homepage. Browsing in all areas can be finely honed and buying books at the site is both simple and secure. Those who want to be notified about new publications and events in particular subject areas can sign up for New Title Text Alerts.

SPECIAL FEATURES

Book Reviews leads to a set of thoughtful reviews by Blackwell's booksellers, listed by subject.

Readers Corner Reading groups may find inspiration in Readers Corner which features a report on the Blackwell's Reading Group's discussion of their book of the month. This page can be reached via the Reviews section.

Student Reading Lists offers access to a database of book lists which can be searched by academic institution and course. This is an excellent idea but content is a little patchy for some institutions as it is dependent on lecturers submitting their booklists to Blackwell's.

Blackwell's Maps Online The outlet for the store's Ordnance Survey agency, is split into two sections: professional and leisure. The professional section of the site covers Siteplan, Landplan and Superplan, while leisure covers the complete OS leisure range with a handy gazetteer search facility. This facility is reached through the Other Blackwell's Products link at the bottom of the homepage.

Ebooks offers an extensive selection of titles across a wide subject range, including many technical and academic texts. The FAQs section is both clear and helpful for those with little or no experience of using ebooks.

Drawing on over 120 years of academic bookselling, the expertise of the Blackwell's website is hard to beat.

www.swotbooks.com
Swotbooks.com
★★★★★ UK 🔒

Although this site can be a little self-consciously cool it certainly succeeds in its aim to help students who are trying to make their book budget stretch further. Searches by ISBN, title and author are easy with a book list to hand or, alternatively, browsing can be narrowed down to suit your course. Well worth a visit for its highly competitive prices and wide-ranging stock which now includes DVDs and CDs.

architecture

www.ribabookshop.com
RIBA Bookshop
★★★ UK 🔒

As the online bookshop for RIBA, the professional association for architects, this site offers details of many essential technical publications. New and important architectural titles are often supported by specially commissioned expert reviews. The site also highlights details of specialist journals, plus newly released and forthcoming titles. Free registration gives access to booklists and catalogues.

art

www.artbook.co.uk
Shipleys
★★★★ UK 🔒

Specialising in old, new, rare and scholarly art books, Shipleys, have been established at 70 Charing Cross Road for over 100 years. The range of books available at this specialist site is hard to beat but browsing can be a little tricky. Click on the initial letter of your chosen category to find the catalogue you want where you will find detailed and thoughtful book descriptions. Book searches for anything that can't be found in the online catalogues can be registered by email and free newsletters are available for a wide range of categories.

art and design

www.magmabooks.com
Magma

★★★★　UK

The cool, metropolitan look of this smart website is a good indication of the type of book to be found in its design and visual arts catalogues. Click on Bookshop for well-chosen and thoughtfully reviewed books in areas such as typography, advertising and web design, as well as fashion, film, architecture and photography. Information on new releases, forthcoming books and specialist magazines can also be found at the site together with details of events at Magma's exhibition space in Clerkenwell.

the arts

www.dancebooks.co.uk
Dancebooks

★★★★　UK

In addition to videos, DVDs and music, this site also features a selection of books on the arts, ranging from ballet and mime to photography and television. Reviews can sometimes be a little perfunctory but the selection is informed and reliable, aimed both at those with an interest in the arts and at those who work in the field.

audiobooks

www.audiobooks.co.uk
The Talking Bookshop

★★★★　UK

This straightforward site is the online home of London's Talking Bookshop which has been open for ten years. It offers an extensive selection of audiobooks on both cassette and CD. Most are abridged but a selection of unabridged books is also available. Ranging from fiction and biography to history and travel, subjects are thoughtfully subdivided for easy browsing and can be searched not only by title, author and keyword but also by reader. Featured titles on both the main homepage and the subject homepages are offered at a 20 per cent discount. The sites main fault lies in its lack of editorial content and although some titles are described most are not.

business and finance

www.profbooks.com
Business and Finance Bookshop

★★★★ UK

The Profbooks.com site houses a variety of specialist bookshops ranging from nuclear engineering to veterinary science and including the Business and Finance Bookshop. Once you have entered the bookshop, click on one of the eight departments to the right of the screen for four expert book recommendations. Each department has its own Top Ten and although the departments have a financial bias, the search facility turns up books on any topic from manufacturing to marketing, from the 20,000 title database. Although the presence of large frames at this site do not make for easy viewing, the authoritative content more than makes up for that.

computers

www.compman.co.uk
Computer Manuals Online Bookstore

★★★★★ UK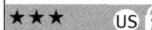

This site is undoubtedly aimed largely at IT professionals but the catalogue does include books for the general reader trying to get to grips with IT with a helpful grading system for each book listed, plus a selection of multimedia and games books. Coverage of computer applications is comprehensive, backed up by the offer of advice, either by email or through the Callback system which offers direct contact with the store's call centre. New publications for the current week are currently promoted with discounts of up to 40 per cent.

cookery

www.books-for-cooks.com
Books for Cooks

★★★ US

Not the Books for Cooks shop in London's Notting Hill but a wide-ranging American bookshop site with an international approach to cookery. Browsing categories include African American, Australasian, and Thai, together with sections on bartending, cooking for one and kosher food. Each month the homepage highlights new books, some with links to recipes, and sometimes features a particular national cuisine with a description of its main characteristics plus a recipe and a selection of books to start you off. The site has an interesting collection of reviews under Appetite for Books Cookbook Reviews.

crime

www.murderone.co.uk
Murder One
★★★★ UK 🔒

Crime aficionados may recognise the name of Maxim Jakubowski's renowned Charing Cross Road store to which this site is attached. A chatty weekly newsletter highlights new crime releases, as well as covering science fiction, fantasy, romance and true crime. Maxim's sharp and witty reviews spotlight more obscure crime novels alongside the pick of the bestsellers. The catalogues are by subject and cover newer titles, although the London shop can be contacted by email for backlist, second-hand and out of print books. A juicy set of crime links is included.

drama

www.samuelfrench-london.co.uk
Samuel French
★★★★ UK

Established in London as theatre booksellers, play publishers and play leasing agents since 1830, the Samuel French shop is an excellent resource for students and drama enthusiasts alike. Theatregoers should visit London Theatre for a listing of what's on where, accompanied by details of relevant play scripts. Catalogues ranging from audition material, speech training, and costume to circus and theatre history can be found in Theatre Booksellers. The site is not secure but orders are accepted by phone, fax or post. Outstanding in its expertise, the site's only drawback is the tiny font used for its text.

film and drama

www.stageplays.com
The Internet Theatre Bookshop
★★★ UK 🔒

This simple, straightforward site carries extensive catalogues of books on the performing arts but is particularly strong on drama and film. A wide range of new and second-hand books on writing techniques for both film and television, screenplays and performance texts are listed, as well as the more usual biographies and books on cinema and theatre history. Playwrights can join a forum and find details of competitions on the Playwrights' Noticeboard by clicking on Playwrights on the Web.

foreign languages

www.grantandcutler.com
Grant and Cutler
★★★★★ UK

Long-established as the UK's expert foreign language booksellers, Grant and Cutler now have all their catalogues, ranging from dictionaries to new foreign fiction, available online. Editorial content is a little thin but the catalogues are extensive, backed up with an offer to track down any foreign language material not included in them. Foreign films, on both video and DVD, are featured in the World Cinema Catalogue. The site is not secure so best to order by phone, fax or post.

gambling

www.gamblingbooks.co.uk
High Stakes
★★★★ UK 🔒

From baccarat to spread betting, this attractive, clearly laid-out site covers books on every aspect of gambling. Relevant new titles are highlighted on category home pages, each of which offers a newsletter to keep you up to date on new publications. The site also includes a variety of links to online betting sites including poker games, bookmakers and spread betting sites.

gardening

www.gardenbooks.freeserve.co.uk
Garden Books by Post
★★★★ UK

This site takes a no-frills approach to gardening books concentrating on confident and often detailed recommendations rather than fancy graphics. It offers a biannual catalogue, details of new and forthcoming titles and a selection of special offers. A list of useful gardening links rounds off this pleasing site. Click Contact for ordering details, as books cannot be ordered online.

gay and lesbian

www.gaystheword.co.uk
Gay's the Word

★★★  UK

Although the range of books reviewed at this site is quite limited, the reliability of its recommendations makes it well worth a visit. Only books that the staff have read and enjoyed are featured on the site but they are happy to deal with queries about other books and can be contacted by email at their London shop. The site is not secure but orders are accepted by phone, fax or post. There is a useful set of links to other gay and lesbian sites.

genealogy

www.ffhs.co.uk
Family History Books

★★★★  UK

Run by the Federation of Family History Societies, this site is arranged as if it were an exhibition hall with a Foyer, a Main Hall, an Enquiry Desk and a set of publishers' and local history societies' Stands. Each stand has a homepage offering information about the society or publisher and listing the contact details while the main hall lists all the stands at the site. The site is easily navigable with lots of help on offer should you need. It offers a comprehensive set of books for genealogists and local historians but if you're after anything in particular you'll need to know which stand to enter as searches are confined to stands.

history

www.historybookshop.com
History Bookshop.com

★★★★★  UK

This imaginative, well-organised site reflects the passion of the small group of enthusiasts who run it. The bookshop departments are split by period but also spill over into related categories such as historical fiction, art history, military and maritime history and genealogy. Click on the title of featured books to view a well-chosen list of related titles. The site also includes articles and timelines that can be drawn together with a list of recommended books for particular periods by using the Themes button. There are generous discounts on books featured on the home page. This is a site for history devotees that is exciting enough to make a few converts.

law

www.hammickslegal.com
Hammicks Legal Bookshops
★★★★★ UK 🔒

Hammicks Legal Bookshops' reputation for wide-ranging stock and expert advice is borne out by this simple, well-designed website. Features include details of essential legal titles due to be published over the coming year, a free email newsletter with reviews of forthcoming titles and a set of useful links to professional legal sites. Catalogue searches produce full bibliographic details of books found.

medical

www.bmjbookshop.com
BMJ Bookshop
★★★★ UK 🔒

Extensive catalogues of medical books can be searched using the comprehensive index of the British Medical Association bookshop site. A host of books on related issues of interest to medical professionals, such as advice on education or welfare and benefits, can also be found through the associated subject index. The site can be slow but its content is authoritative enough to reward a little patience.

music

www.musicbooksrus.com
Music Books r Us
★★★★ UK 🔒

There are no fancy frills incorporated into this specialist site which relies on its comprehensive range of popular music books to speak for itself. Graphics have been deliberately avoided to speed up the searching of categories from Big Bands to New Age Music. Searches can also be made by author, title or artist and there is a small selection of out of print titles backed up by a free book search service.

natural history

www.nhbs.co.uk
Natural History Bookshop
★★★★ UK 🔒

This natural history bookshop with a strong environmental bias carries a wide selection of books on subjects ranging from palaeontology and evolution, to sustainable development. Featured books in each department are supported by the option to view lists of related titles. The site can also be browsed by geographical area. Don't be tempted to skip the first time visitors page which really will help you to get the most out of this specialist site.

pets

www.petbookshop.com
Pet Book Shop
★★★★ UK

This straightforward, comprehensive site can be browsed by subject, from dogs to exotic pets, or searched by title and author. Each browsing area contains a careful selection of new titles with the option to search for more books on that particular subject. Good use is made of reviews from specialist magazines to support the site's recommendations.

politics

www.politicos.co.uk
Politico's
★★★★★ UK

From fiction, both by and about politicians, to constituency profiles by way of speeches, biography, history and satire, Politico's run the entire gamut of books on politics.

Navigation and design are both straightforward although the light coloured font used in the menu bar can be a little hard on the eyes. Bestsellers and new titles are listed on each category homepage with helpful cross-referencing to related categories displayed to the right of the page. The site offers an exceptionally well chosen selection of books coupled with every political artefact you could wish for, from a Trust Me I'm a Civil Servant mug to cartoons. Signed editions and second-hand books are also available.

science fiction, fantasy and horror

www.andromedabook.co.uk/acatalog
Andromeda
★★★★ UK

The online arm of the long-established specialist Birmingham store is squarely aimed at collectors and enthusiasts. The site map is a good place to start for anyone seeking out particular areas of interest. Collectors have their own corner for rare books and small specialist publishers such as Owlswick Press are well represented. There's also a wide selection of signed copies on offer. Although somewhat visually unexciting, Andromeda makes up for it with an abundance of handpicked books guaranteed to appeal to the science fiction connoisseur.

sport

www.sportsbooksdirect.co.uk
Sports Books Direct

★★★★ UK

A nice clean, straightforward site which features six hotly tipped sports books due for imminent release on its homepage. Browsing is by sport with recommendations for the chosen sport plus the option to refine the search further. Signed copies of a small selection of books are available and prices are competitive.

transport

www.motorbooks.co.uk
Motor Books

★★★★★ UK

Despite its very specific name, Motor Books carries a wide range of railway, military, maritime and aviation books, covering the whole gamut of transport and often extending into history. The level of expertise is apparent in the subdivision of the sections and the multitude of books on offer. The railway section, for instance, offers over 40 different subject areas comprising over 6,000 titles in all. Classic and Sports Car, *Motorsport and Classic Cars* magazines review several new books for the site each month, all of them archived and easily accessible. Simple and quick to navigate, this site reflects the accumulated knowledge and enthusiasm of its parent shop, established in London over 50 years ago.

travel

www.stanfords.co.uk
Stanfords

★★★★ UK 🔒

Stanfords's Covent Garden bookshop has long been established as a centre of expertise for maps and travel books, and although both speed and navigation can occasionally disappoint, the content of this smart website only enhances that reputation. The site may be browsed by area of special interest such as diving or climbing books, or by location, and it is in the drop-down selection of cities and countries that navigation can become tricky. However, once the destination has been reached, both the well-chosen selection of books, covering all aspects of travel from guides to travel writing, and the review coverage, make the journey worthwhile. The We've Been There feature, in which the well travelled staff road-test guides and maps, is particularly useful.

rare, antiquarian and second-hand books

If you've ever tried to find a book that's gone out of print, you'll be familiar with the frustrations of such a trade. The internet offers the perfect solution with sites linked to specialist booksellers throughout the world . Collectors of antiquarian books are also well catered for with sites offering an array of extensive catalogues and links to international dealers.

www.abebooks.co.uk			
Advanced Book Exchange			
Overall rating: ★ ★ ★ ★ ★			
Classification:	Ecommerce	Readability:	★ ★ ★ ★
Updating:	Daily	Content:	★ ★ ★ ★
Navigation:	★ ★ ★ ★ ★	Speed:	★ ★ ★ ★
UK 🔒			

With its international network of over 8,000 independent specialist booksellers offering rare, out-of-print and second-hand books, ABE is widely recognised as one of the best sites for collectors and those tracking elusive books. A trip to Help Central module, reached from the Help icon at the top right of the screen, will orient novices. Its animated demonstrations may help the unconfident but they are somewhat lengthy and the text equivalents are equally thorough. The simple main homepage offers a taster for the features reached through The Reading Room, such as Collectables, the Featured Author of the month and literary news. Searches are fast, accurate and can be restricted to country through the Advanced Search option. Subject headings for browsing have been carefully thought through with sub-divisions to narrow the focus. Descriptions of books are aimed firmly at the collector with priority given to precise physical characteristics. Some books may be bought through ABE, although others must be bought direct from the bookseller. There is a handy currency converter for prices.

SPECIAL FEATURES

BookSleuth is for those who have forgotten a particular title or an author. Post as much information as you can on the Booksleuth noticeboard and wait for a reply. Recently Solved is also well worth a visit.

Collectables This monthly feature showcases rare books and first editions.

Glossary Demystifies terms used in book descriptions.

OTHER FEATURES

If the search engine fails to find a book, ABE members can register it on their own Wants list. The list will be matched against ABE's twice-daily updated inventory and an email sent out when the book is found. Membership is free and you can join in the Information box on the homepage .

With a network of over 8,000 independent booksellers, the Advanced Book Exchange offers an excellent chance of tracking down even the most elusive book.

www.worldbookdealers.com
World Book Dealers

Overall rating: ★ ★ ★ ★ ★			
Classification:	Ecommerce	**Readability:**	★ ★ ★ ★ ★
Updating:	Daily	**Content:**	★ ★ ★ ★ ★
Navigation:	★ ★ ★ ★	**Speed:**	★ ★ ★ ★ ★

UK 🔒

A glance at the prices displayed in the catalogues of this elegant site will confirm that this is a place for serious antiquarian and rare book collectors. With its international directory of handpicked specialist book dealers, Worldbookdalers.com provides a forum for both buyers and sellers. The careful thought that has gone into the organisation of the smart homepage, with its Featured Dealer, Special Selection, news roundup, erudite feature article and list of recently acquired dealer catalogues, is reflected throughout the site. Each of the smart red navigation buttons at the top of the page has drop-down menus which lead speedily to the chosen feature. Helpful tips are displayed alongside search boxes. Descriptions of books are precise, placing the book in its historical context as well as detailing its physical characteristics. Wherever possible content pages are supplemented by relevant links, either to material within the site or to other sites. Security of all personal information is guaranteed.

SPECIAL FEATURES

Editorial The editorial content of this site is of a particularly high standard with contributions from acknowledged experts and the enthusiastic in-house team. Articulate and well-researched articles are often scholarly without being stuffy, ranging from accounts of important British Library acquisitions to fundraising bashes, while interviews allow the experts to speak for themselves. There's a small selection of essays on collecting, plus reviews of books devoted to the subject. All editorial content is archived and easily accessible.

Dealers Individual dealers are listed in a directory which can be searched by speciality. Dealers' homepages describe their history, their particular area of expertise and list their catalogues, together with any editorial content available in the site's archives. Contact details, including a link to the dealer's own website, are also included. A search option is provided for the dealer's stock on the right-hand side of the screen. Dealers' homepages can be reached from the Find a Dealer option on the Dealers menu, from catalogue listings or from search results.

Libraries Visit this area for listings of rare book libraries, supplemented by complementary features from the World Book Dealer archive plus details of relevant events and links to the libraries' websites.

Resources includes links to sites offering specialist services such as conservation and digital libraries. There's also a useful glossary and the opportunity to subscribe to WorldBookDealers' free newsletter.

Rich in expert editorial content, this stylish, well-organised site provides an excellent forum for both rare-book collectors and dealers.

www.alibris.com
Alibris

Overall rating: ★ ★ ★ ★			
Classification: Ecommerce		**Readability:**	★ ★ ★ ★ ★
Updating: Unclear		**Content:**	★ ★ ★ ★
Navigation: ★ ★ ★		**Speed:**	★ ★ ★ ★

US 🔒

This fresh-looking site uses a network of booksellers to supplement its stocks of rare and second-hand books. Click on Articles and Features for a wide range of chatty recommendations. The Alibris archives are well worth searching for interesting articles on particular themes and there are lots of collectors' stories to explore from the Look What I Found box on the archive pages. The Sellers part of the site is worth dipping into for more personal recommendations. Visit Collectors to find homepages for first editions, rare, signed and illustrated books. The search box is rather elusive in this area but can be found by clicking on Search at the bottom of the page. The site also includes films and music.

This friendly site is well worth a visit both for recommendations and to track down rare and second-hand books.

OTHER SITES OF INTEREST

Resources for Booksellers and Book Collectors
www.2nd-hand-books.co.uk

Search this simple site for the kind of information that slips thorough everyone else's net, such as a selection of facsimiles of author's signature, useful for those who want to authenticate signed copies. Other handy features include links to bookbinders and tutorials on book conservation, a free email group for collectors, dealers and librarians and a list of UK-based booksearchers. Navigation is about as easy as it gets.

book clubs

Before the 1995 collapse of the Net Book Agreement, which had previously given publishers the right to set the retail price of books, the only way to buy books at discounted prices was to join a book club. Book clubs have adapted to the change by diversifying into specialist areas and offering special paperback editions of books still available only in hardback on the High Street. Several of the clubs reviewed here back up their internet sites with a monthly print magazine which you can browse in the old-fashioned way.

www.booksdirect.co.uk
Books Direct

Overall rating: ★ ★ ★ ★			
Classification: Book Club		**Readability:**	★ ★ ★ ★
Updating: Monthly		**Content:**	★ ★ ★ ★
Navigation: ★ ★ ★ ★		**Speed:**	★ ★ ★ ★

UK 🔒

With their attractive introductory offers and discounted prices, BCA's book club advertisements will be familiar to most UK newspaper and magazine readers. Books Direct is the online arm of BCA and hosts a set of subject-related book clubs, listed below. Individual membership is required to gain full access to each of the club sites, but the umbrella site offers a flavour of what's on offer with a small selection of featured titles, book excerpts and author interviews. Introductory offers for clubs are best explored through the category box at the top left of the screen as several clubs accessible from here aren't included on the logo bar below it. Some club sites, such as World Books, the Arts Guild and the Mystery and Thriller Club, offer a preview for non-members.

Club sites share a uniform, simple format with a navigation bar across the top of the screen, site contents along the left and a set of featured books which changes every month. Although the clubs are subject-related, a range of books from other categories can be browsed from the Search and Category boxes in the top right-hand corner. Membership is simple and secure through the How You Get It screen, but it's worth reading the small print in the membership section of the What We've Got page. If you join you'll be signing up to a minimum annual purchase plus agreeing to notify the club if you don't want to buy the editor's monthly choice. Members receive a print magazine, a password giving them full access to the site plus the introductory offer.

BCA BOOK CLUBS

Mango is aimed squarely at Bridget Jones fans, featuring authors such as Marian Keyes and Jill Mansell alongside Jamie Oliver and Nigella Lawson, with a fair amount of bright and breezy editorial content.

QPD offers a wide range of advance paperback editions of hardback books. The emphasis is on popular literary authors such as John Irving, Zadie Smith and Alison Weir. Rich in editorial content, the site has a wide range of reviews, interviews and book excerpts.

Taste covers popular cookery books and includes a few editorial features along with the month's book selection on the homepage. Taste members receive a privilege card with their introductory package, entitling them to a variety of food-related discounts plus a monthly special offer.

Books for Children has recommendations by age range.

World Books concentrates on delivering bestsellers at discounted prices in a wide range of categories and includes a Pick of the Week in addition to the monthly selections. There is some overlap with the featured titles and content of the QPD site.

Fantasy and SF Book Club offers a selection of related software at discounted prices in conjunction with the Home Software World club site.

Mystery and Thriller Club focuses on bestsellers with a few interviews, excerpts, features and some brief biographical sketches.

TSP is the non-fiction equivalent of QPD and features one monthly fiction selection. There are a rich variety of features including thumbnail portraits of authors linked to their books, plus encouragement to send in a 250-word rant on any subject that particularly incenses you. Amusing examples from fellow ranters can be found on the site. This site can be reached from the Books Direct homepage by choosing the biographies, sciences and nature, or reference category selections, although it covers much more than that.

Escape lives up to its name by offering a wide range of holiday reading, from sagas to thrillers. Editorial content is minimal although reviews are long enough to get a good idea of what the book is about. To reach this site, select historical romances from the category box on the Books Direct page.

The Arts Guild is one of the liveliest of the BCA sites and covers art, photography and design. In addition to articles, book reviews and interviews it also has reviews of major London exhibitions plus a few regional events. The Galleries Guide is an extensive list of British galleries, and Arts Update takes you to a daily updated page of national and international arts news. All three arts events sites are supported by links to relevant websites. This site can be found by choosing the art category on the Books Direct page.

Ancient and Medieval History Book Club, **History Guild**, the **Military and Aviation Book Society** and the **Railway Club** sites all follow the same format. The club magazine for each site can be browsed by category from the left-hand side of the screen. Descriptions of featured books are clear and detailed but there is little else in the way of editorial content.

Each club can be reached through its own category on the Books Direct page.

A linked set of book clubs which covers just about every area of interest.

www.redhouse.co.uk
The Red House

Overall rating: ★ ★ ★ ★			
Classification:	Book Club	**Readability:**	★ ★ ★ ★
Updating:	Monthly	**Content:**	★ ★ ★ ★
Navigation:	★ ★ ★ ★	**Speed:**	★ ★ ★ ★ ★

UK 🔒

The choice of books at this site reflects 30 years of children's bookselling expertise gained both at the Red House bookshop in Oxfordshire and their long-established mail order book club. Books are arranged by age group and navigation is quick and simple. In keeping with the Red House's book club status, prices are very low but the usual monthly commitment to buy a minimum number of books does not apply.

SPECIAL FEATURES

The Red House has a particularly well-chosen set of links for parents which, although it includes several commercial sites, also lists links to charities such as Parentalk, aimed at injecting fun into parenthood, and Mumsnet, set up by a group of mothers to share tips on parenting.

An expertly chosen selection of children's books at bargain prices.

OTHER SITES OF INTEREST

Bol
www.bol.com

Once Amazon's closest rival in the UK, Bol restructured its operations in 2002 and is now a book club offering a wide range of discounted books. Some are special Bol paperback editions of recently published hardbacks. Book of the month choices offer features such as excerpts, author interviews and biographical details but other than that content is restricted to review coverage. Quick and easy to navigate this is a site worth visiting for bargains although membership is required to take advantage of them.

The Good Book Guide
www.thegoodbookguide.co.uk

Packed with reviews and features, The Good Book Guide's monthly print magazine has subscribers worldwide and while the website's content doesn't quite match up to the magazine it's still worth a visit for those who want a flavour of what the organisation is about. Magazine subscribers are entitled to up to 40 per cent discount on selected books and a free copy of the magazine is on offer should you decide to subscribe to the website's newsletter. Visit What We're Reading for wide-ranging and knowledgeable recommendations from the Good Book Guide's staff. Author's Choices' features a selection of favourite books reviewed by writers such as Liza Picard, Penelope Lively and Andrew Motion. The donation of 5 per cent of the cover price to the National Library for the Blind is a nice touch.

Chapter 02

authors

author and fan sites

Lots of authors have cottoned on to the idea of having a website these days and if they haven't, their publishers have arranged one for them. More interesting, however, are the many fan sites set up by enthusiasts who post news, reviews, links to articles and interviews, together with notice boards, chat rooms and a host of other features. Fan sites tend to come and go depending on the time and energy available to maintain them, but where appropriate we've sought them out as an alternative to rather bland official sites.

The reviews in this section include a selection of sites devoted to classic authors such as Jane Austen, with two sites for Shakespeare, one aimed at students, the other at those with a more general interest, together with some current bestselling writers. There are some notable exceptions, Louis de Bernières, for instance, seems to be a little bashful as far as the internet is concerned and fans have not obliged, but in the next section you'll find a set of sites to help you track down information on authors not included below.

Sites in this section are listed in alphabetical order.

martin amis

http://martinamis.albion.edu
The Martin Amis Web

Overall rating: ★ ★ ★ ★ ★			
Classification: Fan Site		**Readability:**	★ ★ ★ ★
Updating: Monthly		**Content:**	★ ★ ★ ★ ★
Navigation: ★ ★ ★ ★		**Speed:**	★ ★ ★ ★ ★

US

Put together by James Diedrick, an American Professor of Humanities and author of *Understanding Martin Amis*, this well-researched website is devoted to all aspects of Martin Amis's work. The homepage provides links to interviews, essays, new books and news about Amis. Neatly organised, each section homepage has a set of options singled out for special interest, to the right of the screen. Subjects covered range from biographical information to a list of interviews and include a section on Amis and postmodernism. The site has a Discussion Web which can be viewed before signing up. There's a direct link to amazon.com.

SPECIAL FEATURES

Affinities lists links to information on authors who have influenced Amis such as Vladimir Nabokov and Jane Austen.

Bookshelf includes a set of Amis's recommendations as well as listing books by and about him.

Neatly organised and exhaustively researched, this site is an excellent source of information on Martin Amis.

margaret atwood

www.owtoad.com
Margaret Atwood Reference Site

Overall rating: ★ ★ ★ ★			
Classification: Official Site		**Readability:**	★ ★ ★
Updating: Sporadically		**Content:**	★ ★ ★ ★ ★
Navigation: ★ ★ ★ ★		**Speed:**	★ ★ ★ ★

CA

With a good deal of gentle humour, Margaret Atwood and her staff aim to provide answers at this site to any questions either her fans or researchers are likely to ask. This is an attractive site but finding your way around can be a little challenging. It's best explored through The Table of Contents reached by clicking the book icon once you have entered the main site. There are a number of essays, reviews, lectures and observations by Atwood which will provide a treat for her many fans, from a charming memoir of her gardening efforts, found in Life and Times, to a lecture on writing poetry, given at the Hay-on-Wye literary festival in On Writing. Aficionados will want to search From the Desk of Margaret Atwood which contains some charming cartoons inspired by book tours, although the site's graphics in this section are a little gimmicky. That said, this is both a pleasing and informative site.

The gentle humour and exhaustive content of this site combine to make it a treat for Margaret Atwood fans.

jane austen

www.austen.com
Austen.com

Overall rating: ★ ★ ★ ★ ★			
Classification: Fan Site		**Readability:**	★ ★ ★ ★ ★
Updating: Regularly		**Content:**	★ ★ ★ ★
Navigation: ★ ★ ★ ★ ★		**Speed:**	★ ★ ★ ★

UK

The homepage of this neatly designed website clearly explains how it all works. As well as providing access to Jane Austen's novels online, there is a collection of carefully chosen links to other sites including The Regency on the Web which offers a detailed historical context for Austen's work. Each novel is briefly introduced and links to the texts are presented chapter by chapter. A detailed essay on *Lovers' Vows* helpfully explains the historical significance of the play in the *Mansfield Park* entry. Off-Line Jane Austen Resources has links to societies throughout the world and includes a list of biographies and books on the Regency period.

SPECIAL FEATURES

The Derbyshire Writers' Guild is devoted to creative writing based on Austen's characters and novels. Contributions are welcome and stories are archived. This part of the site also houses the lively discussion board, Jane Austen's Tea Room.

A well-laid out site which offers links to sites devoted to Jane Austen's work and times plus a lively discussion board and a creative writing community.

the brontës

www.bronte.org.uk
Brontë Parsonage Museum

Overall rating: ★ ★ ★ ★ ★			
Classification: Information		**Readability:**	★ ★ ★
Updating: Unclear		**Content:**	★ ★ ★ ★ ★
Navigation: ★ ★ ★ ★		**Speed:**	★ ★ ★ ★

UK 🔒

The online home of the Brontë Parsonage Museum is decorated with pictures of the museum and the surrounding Yorkshire moors. The section labelled The Brontës begins with an essay placing the family in its historical context and includes a detailed chronology under Brief History, together with a biographical essay and a family tree. Lengthy synopses of the sisters' novels include commentary on structure and theme. Audio tapes, videos, critical guides and biographies can all be found in the shop alongside the novels, and the site also includes details of how to join the Brontë Society. There are useful links to other Brontë sites. Although simple to navigate, the small font used can make reading a little hard. A relaunch is planned and a sneak preview can be found via a link on the current site's homepage.

SPECIAL FEATURES

The Museum Guided Tour is effectively a tour of the Brontë family home complete with a selection of photographs and a commentary exploring the family history.

Offers a tour of the Brontë home from your own armchair.

raymond chandler

http://home.usit.net/~mossr
The Raymond Chandler Website

Overall rating: ★ ★ ★ ★

Classification:	Fan Site	**Readability:**	★ ★ ★ ★
Updating:	Regularly	**Content:**	★ ★ ★ ★ ★
Navigation:	★ ★ ★ ★	**Speed:**	★ ★ ★ ★

US

This tribute to the father of the American hard-boiled crime novel features a number of essays, including an introduction to *The Big Sleep*, and a set of links to academic papers on Chandler and his work, under Criticism and Scholarship. Those interested in biographical details may be disappointed by Chandler's Life which is a simple timeline rather than an essay. In Features, Chandler's Los Angeles offers a set of illustrated short essays on locations and real life characters in the novels although, sadly, the photographs of Raymond Chandler Square, inaugurated as an historical monument in 1994, seem no longer to be accessible. Chandler's Works includes an essay on his early poetry plus Chandler's Movies, which has some great poster reproductions.

SPECIAL FEATURES

Cracking the Cassidy Case reached from Features, this is a dissection of a real life murder which was referred to in *The High Window*.

Chandlerisms is a page of favourite quotations, hard to read without summoning up a trench-coated, cigarette-smoking Humphrey Bogart. It can be found in the Features pages.

Dedicated to the father of hard-boiled American crime writing, this site offers a few surprises including Chandler's early poetry alongside the well-loved quotations.

geoffrey chaucer

http://geoffreychaucer.org			
Geoffreychaucer.org			
Overall rating: ★ ★ ★ ★			
Classification: Directory	**Readability:**	★ ★ ★	
Updating: Unclear	**Content:**	★ ★ ★ ★ ★	
Navigation: ★ ★ ★ ★ ★	**Speed:**	★ ★ ★ ★ ★	
US			

Run by David Wilson-Okamura, an academic specialising in Medieval Studies, this attractive site provides a useful shortcut to the best of the proliferation of Chaucerian sites on the web. Click on a category on the red bar to the left of the screen to display a page of links to relevant sites. Each site is accurately but succinctly described so that you know what to expect when you get there. Category pages feature a carefully chosen book and you can link to either amazon.com or amazon.co.uk to buy it. Chaucer's background, biography, language and bibliography are all included as categories, together with links to online publications of *The Canterbury Tales*, teaching resources and commentaries. There is also a link to a sister site on Virgil.

SPECIAL FEATURES

Links lists a set of general sites together with a set of links to scholarly Medieval Studies sites.

This expertly assembled directory site leads you through the maze of Chaucerian websites to the pick of the crop.

charles dickens

www.fidnet.com/~dap1955/dickens/index.html			
The Charles Dickens Page			
Overall rating: ★ ★ ★ ★			
Classification: Fan Site	**Readability:**	★ ★ ★ ★	
Updating: Regularly	**Content:**	★ ★ ★ ★ ★	
Navigation: ★ ★ ★ ★	**Speed:**	★ ★ ★ ★	
US			

This site is a must for fans and scholars. Each section is devoted to a particular aspect of Dickens's life, work and times, ranging from an introduction to his novels to thumbnail sketches of his illustrators and an account of his American lecture tours. Content is dense but well organised with links to relevant information appearing below the left-hand menu and embedded in the text.

SPECIAL FEATURES

The Novels have a page each with a link to the online text at the top of the page, followed by a brief synopsis, an index of principal characters and links to relevant websites.

Characters is an A–Z listing of Dickens's characters.

Dickens's London is a brief essay on Victorian London with links to relevant websites.

Dickens & Christmas examines his influence over Christmas celebrations.

This attractive, organised site is packed with information.

sir arthur conan doyle

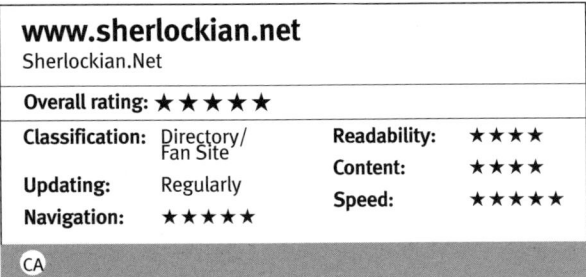

www.sherlockian.net
Sherlockian.Net

Overall rating: ★ ★ ★ ★ ★			
Classification:	Directory/ Fan Site	Readability:	★ ★ ★ ★
Updating:	Regularly	Content:	★ ★ ★ ★
Navigation:	★ ★ ★ ★ ★	Speed:	★ ★ ★ ★ ★

CA

This well-maintained site is an excellent place to start exploring the world of Sherlock Holmes on the internet. The level of detail should satisfy even the most dedicated fan, with links to the BBC webcam trained on the corner of Baker Street and Marylebone Road plus a painstaking reconstruction of 221b Baker Street. For those with a more general interest, the site offers a well-organised set of links in addition to content such as the View Halloa, a set of introductory essays to each of the Sherlock Holmes stories, a brief biography of Conan Doyle and news of events and additions on its homepage. Links are organised under headings such as Societies and Events, English and Victorian the world of Holmes and Watson, and are also embedded within the site's own content. Access to a variety of online editions of the Holmes stories, is supported by links to sites offering the historical background to each story.

An excellent starting point for fans wanting to explore the best of the many websites devoted to Sherlock Holmes.

jasper fforde

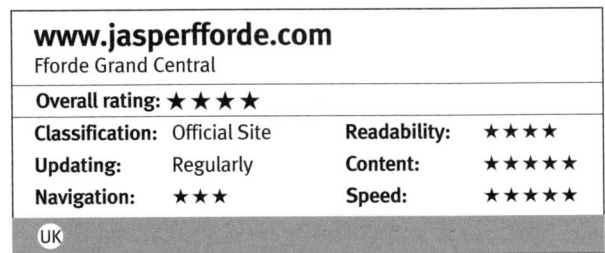

www.jasperfforde.com
Fforde Grand Central

Overall rating: ★ ★ ★ ★			
Classification:	Official Site	Readability:	★ ★ ★ ★
Updating:	Regularly	Content:	★ ★ ★ ★ ★
Navigation:	★ ★ ★	Speed:	★ ★ ★ ★ ★

UK

The content of this website reflects the wacky humour that endears Jasper Fforde's novels, featuring literary sleuth Thursday Next, to his growing band of fans. Although the homepage lists and describes all that's available, the index is a good place to start for first time visitors. Features include the Special Operations website, the Swindon Photograph Album, the Goliath Corporation website, Thursday Next's homepage, plus news, games and forums. The Writing Section is worth a visit for Jasper's guided tour of the site which includes a link to Readers' Contributions.

SPECIAL FEATURES

Jurisfiction contains a glossary for the books plus illustrations that Jasper would have liked to include in his novels.

Pickwick's Calvacade of Fun has lots of humorous games, from literary quizzes to memory tests. Navigation can come unstuck in this section.

Those readers who enjoy Jasper Fforde's particular brand of wackiness will find much to entertain them here.

thomas hardy

www.gettysburg.edu/academics/english/hardy		
Thomas Hardy's World		
Overall rating: ★ ★ ★		
Classification: Academic	Readability:	★ ★ ★
Updating: Unclear	Content:	★ ★ ★ ★
Navigation: ★ ★	Speed:	★ ★ ★
US		

Largely made up of short academic papers, this site has much to offer on Thomas Hardy's life and times, but its navigation is extremely basic and you will find yourself relying on your browser back button to find your way around. From the pretty homepage, with its Dorset thatched cottages, you can visit About Hardy's World for background information about the site, or click on Enter Hardy's World which leads to the main content. Although there are several essays on Hardy's short fiction and poetry, the novels section is surprisingly brief; however, the sections on Hardy's relationship with the land and his historical context more than make up for this. Contexts is particularly strong on class, science, religion and folklore in Hardy's work with the Sister Arts pages devoted to an exploration of Hardy's work in relation to cinema, drama and architecture as well as examining Victorian attitudes to the moral questions posed in his novels. You'll find links to online texts and various Thomas Hardy societies in the Related Web Sites section

Particularly useful for those wanting to explore the cultural and historical contexts of Thomas Hardy's writing.

james joyce

www.2street.com/joyce		
Work in Progress		
Overall rating: ★ ★ ★ ★		
Classification: Fan Site	Readability:	★ ★ ★ ★
Updating: Unclear	Content:	★ ★ ★ ★
Navigation: ★ ★ ★ ★ ★	Speed:	★ ★ ★ ★
IRE		

Although there's much to explore at this site devoted to James Joyce and his work, sections are still under development. Clever use of a single frame makes navigation simple or you can use the links on the friendly homepage which talks you through what's available. Features include academic papers, Joycean maps of Dublin, links to journals and a timeline, plus a set of links to other sites. Links to online texts of Joyce's work are currently broken.

SPECIAL FEATURES

Joycean Multimedia Gallery reached from M-media, includes a short reading by Joyce from Finnegan's Wake, plus the song which inspired the novel's title. You'll need RealPlayer software, downloadable via a link at the site, to hear these audio clips.

Groups includes details of both online and face-to-face discussion groups. There is an extensive list of groups from around the world who meet regularly to discuss Joyce's work.

Although under development, this site is an excellent resource.

stephen king

http://utopianweb.com/king			
Stephen King Website			
Overall rating: ★ ★ ★ ★ ★			
Classification: Fan Site		**Readability:**	★ ★ ★ ★
Updating: Unclear		**Content:**	★ ★ ★ ★
Navigation: ★ ★ ★ ★		**Speed:**	★ ★ ★ ★
US			

Work seems to have ground to a bit of a halt on this smart site, one of the best of the many internet shrines to Stephen King, but it's still well worth a visit. The News page is a little neglected but there's much more to explore here. The Collecting page lists details of limited editions plus short stories included in anthologies and magazines, together with links to interviews. The Media Gallery includes a full transcript of the *60 Minutes* interview, well known to fans. Easily navigable and crammed with information, this site still knocks spots off the official Stephen King website.

SPECIAL FEATURES

Other Links includes film, publishers' and other fan sites, although a few of the publishers' sites have now lapsed. Online articles can be found here and there is a link to the official Stephen King site, worth a visit for up-to-date news.

Postcards of book jackets or pictures of Stephen King can be sent by **email** with music to go with your message.

A mine of information for Stephen King fans.

barbara kingsolver

www.kingsolver.com			
Barbara Kingsolver			
Overall rating: ★ ★ ★			
Classification: Official Site		**Readability:**	★ ★ ★ ★
Updating: Unclear		**Content:**	★ ★ ★
Navigation: ★ ★ ★ ★		**Speed:**	★ ★ ★ ★
US			

Run by the author, this attractive site has a pleasant personal tone. It offers information about Kingsolver's background and interests, together with lengthy answers to questions about her two bestselling books and other topics in the FAQ section. Excerpts are available from her poetry, essays and less well known novels such as *Animal Dreams*. There are suggested discussion points for each of Kingsolver's books in the For Reading Groups section, although some are very brief. There is a snail mail address for contacting the author through her publisher in FAQ, although she does warn her readers that she is unable to answer all questions individually.

SPECIAL FEATURES

The News section offers updates on new writing projects plus information on the Bellwether Prize, complete with a link to the Bellwether site.

This simple website will interest reading groups and fans wanting to learn more about Barbara Kingsolver's background.

gabriel garcia marquez

www.libyrinth.com/gabo			
Gabriel Garcia Marquez			
Overall rating: ★ ★ ★ ★			
Classification: Fan Site		**Readability:**	★ ★ ★ ★
Updating: Unclear		**Content:**	★ ★ ★ ★ ★
Navigation: ★ ★ ★ ★ ★		**Speed:**	★ ★ ★ ★
US			

Part of Modern World, a small suite of literary sites which includes Umberto Eco, Thomas Pynchon and Samuel Beckett, this beautifully illustrated site is a shrine to the great Colombian Magic Realist novelist, Gabriel Garcia Marquez. A great deal of care has gone into researching the site's rich content which ranges from lengthy synopses of Marquez's work to a full transcript of his Nobel Prize acceptance speech. The navigation bar to the left of the screen leads you to all that the site has to offer. Some pages can be slow to load but the excellent quality of the images contained within them makes it well worth the wait. Other authors in the suite can be found by clicking Authors on the top navigation bar. You can subscribe to The Modern World's free newsletter *Spiral-Bound*, from the bottom of any page.

SPECIAL FEATURES

Biography is a detailed biographical essay on Marquez, complete with the historical background of Colombia, and how it has influenced his work.

Links takes you to a carefully researched set of links to other Marquez and Latin American literature sites including work by Marquez published online. There are a multitude of links to other Marquez websites throughout the site, many of which are not included on this page. The Papers page, for instance, lists links to dissertations and essays available online.

Magical Realism is a brief description of the literary device employed by Marquez and many other Latin American authors, together with links to sites devoted to Magical Realism.

Film has lengthy descriptions and reviews of all films connected with Marquez, including documentaries and TV programmes.

Music lists compositions influenced by Marquez's work with links to relevant sites.

From ardent fans to literature scholars, this site is a magnificent resource for all readers of Gabriel Garcia Marquez.

patrick o'brian

www.wwnorton.com/pob/pobhome.htm	
The Patrick O'Brian Page	
Overall rating: ★ ★ ★ ★	
Classification: Publisher	**Readability:** ★ ★ ★ ★
Updating: Unclear	**Content:** ★ ★ ★
Navigation: ★ ★ ★ ★	**Speed:** ★ ★ ★ ★
ⓤⓢ	

Maintained by Patrick O'Brian's American publishers, W. W. Norton, the content of this site is a little thin but it does act as a gateway to several colourful fan sites devoted to a variety of aspects of O'Brian's work, in addition to hosting a lively discussion forum which is used on a daily basis. A click on the link in the Aubrey/Maturin box on the homepage takes you to a list of O'Brian's novels, including those outside the famous nautical series, which in turn leads to detailed synopses of the books. The other main features of the site can be reached from the top of the homepage. Unfortunately, the newsletter is no longer in production but archives can be browsed through the Newsletter link. A set of discussion questions on *Master and Commander*, *The Yellow Admiral* and the Aubrey/Maturin series as a whole can be found via the Reading Group Guide link.

SPECIAL FEATURES

The Gunroom is a vibrant mailing list run by fans whose passionate enthusiasm for O'Brian's novels spills over into adopting the names of his characters to sign their contributions. No longer maintained by W. W. Norton, The Gunroom is a separate site easily reached from The Patrick O'Brian Page via Links. It's well worth a visit both for its colourful design, and for features such as recommendations for other books, found under The Gunroom Book List, and the Patrick O'Brian Discussion Archives which go back to 1996.

Web Discussion Forum is very much alive and kicking at this site, despite the departure of the newsletter. The forum is used on a daily basis with questions and contributions from fans wanting to debate the historical detail, plot, characters and writing of O'Brian's nautical series. Entries are usually intelligent, knowledgeable and enthusiastic. Guests can post messages at the forum but registration is necessary to edit or delete messages previously posted. Archives are available, although they are extremely slow to download and cannot be searched.

Links This page has been contributed to The Patrick O'Brian Page by The Gunroom. It includes Gibbons Burke's highly regarded directory of O'Brian sites, plus links to maritime museums and societies for fans eager to track down details of nautical history.

A good starting point for fans of Patrick O'Brian's nautical novels in search of fellow enthusiasts and background information.

george orwell

www.k-1.com/orwell
The George Orwell 1903–50

Overall rating: ★ ★ ★ ★			
Classification:	Fan Site	**Readability:**	★ ★ ★
Updating:	Regularly	**Content:**	★ ★ ★ ★ ★
Navigation:	★ ★ ★ ★	**Speed:**	★ ★ ★ ★

US

Dedicated to the author best known for his satirical novels, *1984* and *Animal Farm*, this attractive easily navigable site contains a lengthy biographical essay plus photographs of the author, together with a selection of Orwell's poems, journalism and essays. Detailed synopses of a selection of Orwell's books can be found under Summaries and Interpretations. The Essays section offers a selection of Orwell's journalism ranging from *Notes on Dali* to *Why Socialists Don't Believe in Fun*. Readers are invited to submit their own essays to the Opinions section which includes several academic analyses of Orwell's work. Links to other George Orwell sites are well worth exploring.

Students of Orwell will find the biographical information and detailed book synopses at this site invaluable.

terry pratchett

www.co.uk.lspace.org
The L-Space Web: A Terry Pratchett/Discworld site

Overall rating: ★ ★ ★ ★ ★			
Classification:	Fan Site	**Readability:**	★ ★ ★ ★
Updating:	Regularly	**Content:**	★ ★ ★ ★ ★
Navigation:	★ ★ ★ ★ ★	**Speed:**	★ ★ ★ ★

UK

This well-organised, comprehensive site should please Terry Pratchett's many ardent fans and appears to have the approval of the man himself. The homepage acts as a contents list for the site which includes a detailed biography of Pratchett by his literary agent, interviews and contact details, a collection of articles on his books, information on illustrations and details of news groups. The site is well maintained and designed for ease of use, with a good deal of cross-referencing so that it's hard to miss anything. It includes a set of links to other Pratchett websites throughout the world under Other Resources.

SPECIAL FEATURES

The Pratchett Quote File can be reached from the Terry Pratchett section and consists of quotes taken from Pratchett's contributions to the alt.fan.pratchett newsgroup

Books and Writings features a selection of articles about Pratchett's novels including a collection of annotations for each of the books and a Discworld timeline. This section also includes an online version of *Theatre of Cruelty*, a short story originally commissioned by W H Smith and now unavailable in print form.

Art and Graphics includes a collection of illustrations by Pratchett for the first edition of *The Carpet People*.

Fan Activity is a comprehensive introduction to newsgroups, chatrooms and fan clubs devoted to Pratchett.

Games hosts the subsite, The Discworld Games Pages, which offers tips and hints on playing the Perfect Entertainment CD-Rom games. The Games section also includes the trivia game, Unseen University Challenge, and a downloadable version of the very first Discworld game, based on *The Colour of Magic*, together with a set of links to other games sites.

At the centre of the Terry Pratchett web community, this site combines all the enthusiasm and inventiveness of a fan site with contributions from the man himself.

william shakespeare

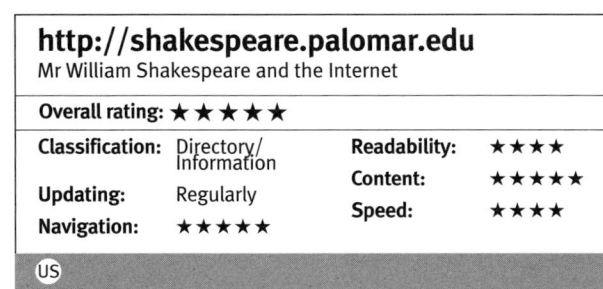

http://shakespeare.palomar.edu
Mr William Shakespeare and the Internet

Overall rating: ★ ★ ★ ★			
Classification:	Directory/Information	**Readability:**	★ ★ ★ ★
Updating:	Regularly	**Content:**	★ ★ ★ ★ ★
Navigation:	★ ★ ★ ★ ★	**Speed:**	★ ★ ★ ★

US

This site aims to pull together the best of the mass of scholarly Shakespearean material available on the internet; a colossal task, but Terry Gray has succeeded in constructing an invaluable site for both academics and enthusiasts. The site includes material that Terry has put together himself, such as a Timeline supported by a family tree and a summary, but it's primarily an annotated directory to the best sites on the web for Shakespeare studies. Attractively presented, the site is easy to use with a navigation bar to the left of the screen highlighting the various categories of information available on the site, ranging from Shakespeare's Life and Times, to information on his Sources. It's well worth reading both the Introduction and the introductory paragraph at the top of each category page which clearly describes the pages contents and gives a quick guide to where to find what. There's a good deal of cross-referencing between pages to help you find what you want. A visit to What's News from the top of the home page indicates the high degree of updating and maintenance at this exhaustive site. All links are accompanied by brief but informed comments on the site's contents.

SPECIAL FEATURES

Life and Times brings together biographical sites including those that deal with the controversial question as to whether Shakespeare was the author of the plays we know him for.

Works provides an index to the many editions of Shakespeare's plays and poetry published on the internet including Charles and Mary Lamb's *Tales from Shakespeare*.

Theatre offers links to sites which deal with the aspects of Shakespearean theatre such as swordplay, costume and music as well as links to London's reconstructed Globe theatre website and other sites throughout the world concerned with the authentic reproduction of Shakespeare's theatre.

Renaissance deals with the historical background of the period and includes links to sites on Shakespeare's contemporaries such as Francis Bacon, John Donne and Edmund Spenser.

Sources provides an index of sites for the Bible, the Classics and Medieval literature, all of which influenced Shakespeare's writing together with links to other sources of historical information helpful in studying his work.

Educational houses links to teaching aids and materials on the internet, designed to be used either online or in the classroom.

Best Sites is made up of the sites rated by Terry Gray as the best on the web and is well worth a visit for a quick, reliable summary of what's available. Its directory mirrors the left-hand navigation bar.

"Other Sites" is headed "sites your mother should have warned you about". Worth visiting for some light relief.

A triumph of organisation and enthusiasm, this excellent site provides a well-informed guide to the mass of Shakespearean information available on the internet.

j. r. r. tolkien

www.lordotrings.com
Lord of the Rings Fanatics Site

Overall rating: ★ ★ ★ ★ ★			
Classification: Fan Site		**Readability:**	★ ★ ★ ★
Updating: Regularly		**Content:**	★ ★ ★ ★ ★
Navigation: ★ ★ ★ ★ ★		**Speed:**	★ ★ ★ ★

US 🔒

This beautifully illustrated site is a shrine to both *The Lord of the Rings* and its author. The opening page offers either a Flash-enabled or non-Flash version – it's worth watching the introductory Full Flash Demo if you already have the software. The clearly laid out homepage lists all that's available and movement between its many features is simple and quick. Creative contributions are invited in the Specials section and there are links to sites selling Tolkien-related items. The Community section list links to games sites, other fan sites, newsgroups and chat rooms. A section devoted to *The Lord of the Rings* movies is also included. Each page offers the chance to vote your favourite Tolkien site with top sites singled out in the Award Winners section.

SPECIAL FEATURES

The Writer includes a 1971 BBC Radio 4 interview with Tolkien about the writing of *Lord of the Rings*.

The Books features a chapter-by-chapter summary of The Lord of the Rings, with a timeline showing which of the main characters were involved in the main events of the book.

Guided Tours offers four 20-minute guided tours of the locations, people, creatures and weapons of Middle-Earth. Each tour consists of illustrated detailed descriptions written in the style of Bilbo Baggins. The four tours are combined in the Complete Tour of Middle Earth and each follows a flexible design with lots of opportunities to shorten the tour or go back on yourself if you choose.

Quest Quiz is divided into six, one for each of the six books which make up *The Lord of the Rings* and includes 111 questions in all. Each quiz is hosted by Bilbo Baggins and the levels of difficulty assigned range from Very Easy to a challenging Impossible.

Arts & Media showcases the work of Greg and Tim Hildebrandt, John Howe, and Ted Nasmith.

Merchandise Shop Items inspired by *The Lord of the Rings*, from Pewter goblets to posters and cards. All purchases made at the site are secure.

Specials contributions are invited for this part of the site which houses games, Flash movies, artwork and writing. To contribute visit Submission Guidelines.

Fanatics Plaza Features include well-frequented discussion forums, and quizzes enable you to earn points and work your way up the Fanatics Plaza ranking hierarchy. You must register as a member to take part but membership is free.

The beautiful artwork, guided tours of Middle Earth and taxing quiz make it a treat for all fans of The Lord of the Rings.

irvine welsh

www.irvinewelsh.com			
irvinewelsh.com			
Overall rating: ★ ★ ★ ★			
Classification: Fan Site		Readability:	★ ★ ★ ★
Updating: Unclear		Content:	★ ★ ★ ★ ★
Navigation: ★ ★ ★ ★ ★		Speed:	★ ★ ★ ★
UK			

Although Irvine Welsh now has an official website which, in true Welsh style, he warns will probably be a passing fad, and there's also a promising fan site called *The Irvine Welsh Hole*, *Spike Magazine*'s homage to one of their favourite authors is still the best Welsh site available. The first half of the site lists links to *Spike*'s own articles while the rest of the page features links to other sites, including the two mentioned above together with reviews, interviews, news articles and film websites. Each link has a description of the associated site's contents and there are direct links to amazon.co.uk or amazon.com to buy either books or videos, all of which are listed.

The best source of information on the internet about the godfather of the new Scottish literature.

jeanette winterson

www.jeanettewinterson.com			
Jeanette Winterson: The Official Site			
Overall rating: ★ ★ ★ ★			
Classification: Official Site		Readability:	★ ★ ★ ★
Updating: Monthly		Content:	★ ★ ★ ★ ★
Navigation: ★ ★ ★ ★ ★		Speed:	★ ★ ★ ★
UK			

Jeanette Winterson's site has a lively, personal feel. In the Reading feature she recommends books from her own reading, plus a monthly article about life in general and her own life in particular, in Monthly Column. The largest section is devoted to Winterson's books with extracts, which can be heard or read, and a synopsis followed by a brief set of questions and answers. Those interested in other aspects of her work besides her writing should visit Multimedia for info on her contributions to theatre, radio and television.

SPECIAL FEATURES

Journalism links to Winterson's work for a variety of publications including *The Guardian*, *The Times* and *The New Yorker*.

Directory is a set of links to websites on all manner of things that have caught Winterson's eye, including a few designated as Mad Sites.

A lively website with a strong personal feel which will please Jeanette Winterson fans.

OTHER SITES OF INTEREST

The Official Robert Burns Site
www.robertburns.org

The official Robert Burns website offers access to the works of the Scottish bard online, complete with a handy pop-up multilingual glossary for the trickier words. There's a small selection of Burns's poetry translated into English for those who find themselves defeated by eighteenth-century Scottish vernacular. The Burns Encyclopedia provides a guide to the poems and their historical background. One of the site's best features is the item on Burns Suppers, which has its own homepage plus poems, toasts and recipes for 25th January. No registration is needed to join in the lively Burns discussion area. The site is part of the Scotweb webring, which exists to promote Scottish goods and services, so there is ample opportunity to buy related products.

John Irving is God
www.geocities.com/irvingophile/Home.html

An offshoot of the John Irving is God Book Club, the chief attraction at this fan site is the lengthy set of questions put to the interview-shy Irving via his publishers, featured in the Q & A pages. Other features include news stories about Irving on the homepage, although it's some time since the site has been updated, and an exhaustive bibliography is still under construction. The navigation of the site is a little haphazard in places and it's best to visit the interviews section from the bottom of Links as it seems to have been missed off the bibliography directory. Links also houses a variety of connections to other Irving websites including the John Irving is God Book Club.

The Samuel Johnson Sound Bite Page
www.samueljohnson.com

Frank Lynch's site offers a concise biography of the man whose many achievements include producing the first dictionary of the English language in 1755. The Timeline summarises Johnson's life and career, while the Books section outlines both his own work and books about him, including James Boswell's classic biography, *The Life of Johnson*. The bulk of the site is made up of quotations illustrating the often irascible but always pithy wit of Dr Johnson, with an enjoyable sampler page, a set of links to some well chosen topic-related quotations, a top twenty of the month and a keyword search facility.

Anniinina's Toni Morrison Page
www.luminarium.org/contemporary/tonimorrison

Likely to be of interest to students of Toni Morrison, this attractive site gathers together online references to Morrison's work, including many from the *African American Review*. Click on one of the book titles adorning the tree in the centre of the page, or use the menu to the left to display a page of links to reviews, essays and articles, ranging from academic papers to items of more general interest such as reviews from *The New York Times*. The Biographies option offers a selection of short biographical essays while Bibliographies takes you to the Carnegie Library's list of critical texts. Other Sources lists contact details for the author together with a link to the Toni Morrison Society.

Plathonline.com
www.plathonline.com

This site has been long under construction but Emily Pollard has finally succeeded in her aim to provide a well organised and easily accessible directory to the multitude of websites on Sylvia Plath. The Complete Link List is split in to twelve areas and includes links to sites offering educational resources, a section on Ted and Frieda Hughes, links to foreign sites, audio and video sites plus online texts of Plath's Poetry, although many of these are available at plathonline under Poetry. Some of the websites listed in the full and small/incomplete sites take a very personal stand on the Hughes/Plath debate but the site gathers together many of the better entries on the internet about Plath including articles from *Salon*, *The Guardian* and the BBC. Vist Weblog for new websites not yet entered in the directory.

finding information about authors

Space does not permit a comprehensive list of sites devoted to individual authors, which would probably require a book to itself, but the sites listed below should help plug any gaps. Some are databases of information about authors associated with particular areas of literature, such as crime writing or the nineteenth century, while others work as a directory of links to author sites, mailing lists and chat rooms. All are straightforward and easy to use.

http://books.guardian.co.uk/authors/ 0,6110,94875,00.html		
Guardian Unlimited: The Authors		
Overall rating: ★ ★ ★ ★		
Classification: Database	**Readability:**	★ ★ ★
Updating: Unclear	**Content:**	★ ★ ★ ★ ★
Navigation: ★ ★ ★ ★	**Speed:**	★ ★ ★ ★ ★
UK		

Part of *The Guardian*'s Books website, these pages meet the same high standard as the rest of the site. Ranging from Peter Ackroyd to Emile Zola via Iain Banks, Richard Dawkins, Nick Hornby and George Orwell, to name but a few, each author listed in the A–Z directory has a page containing brief biographical details, what the critics think and intelligent suggestions for what to read next and why. To the left of each entry there are links to the author's homepage, other articles, book excerpts and reviews, where appropriate. Scroll down to On this Site to find links to *Guardian* articles about the author.

Clearly laid out author biographies are backed up by links to other relevant sites plus articles and reviews from Guardian Unlimited's extensive books pages.

http://www.bastulli.com
Bastulli Mystery Library

Overall rating: ★ ★ ★ ★			
Classification:	Database	Readability:	★ ★ ★ ★
Updating:	Unclear	Content:	★ ★ ★ ★ ★
Navigation:	★ ★ ★ ★	Speed:	★ ★ ★ ★

US

There's lots to explore at this site, not least it's amusingly gruesome graphics. Devoted to crime fiction, from the hard-boiled American variety to classic whodunnit, the site has reviews, interviews, categorised lists of crime books and a large bank of information about authors. The content has been pulled together by two ardent crime fans from a variety of internet sources and rewritten to match their own format. It's easy to find your way around using the bright red navigation bar and despite those bloodcurdling graphics which include dancing skeletons and revolving skulls, response is speedy.

SPECIAL FEATURES
Search the **A-Z Index of Authors** to find your favourite crime writer, from Jeffery Deaver to Barbara Vine. Author profiles include biographical details, plot synopses, the crime category to which they belong and links to other sites.

An excellent resource for information on authors.

www.catharton.com/authors
Catharton.com

Overall rating: ★ ★ ★ ★			
Classification:	Directory/ Information	Readability:	★ ★ ★ ★
Updating:	Daily	Content:	★ ★ ★ ★ ★
Navigation:	★ ★ ★ ★	Speed:	★ ★ ★ ★ ★

UK

For links to information on authors from Kafka to Ruth Rendell, this simple site is hard to beat. Each author entry is clearly laid out with a list of links to websites, message boards, mailing lists and chat rooms, sometimes accompanied by bibliographical lists. As the site is something of a one-man band, there's lots of encouragement to contribute to it by submitting articles on favourite authors, adding links to author entries and offering feedback. Pages on musicians, artists and film directors, can be found by clicking on the C icon at the top left-hand corner of the screen. Content and presentation at this site are excellent.

SPECIAL FEATURES

Message Boards are worth visiting although you'll have to register to contribute. There are several genre message boards ranging from science fiction to romance plus a few more general boards but the more interesting exchanges tend to take place in the author forums.

An entertaining site which specialises in information on crime writers and crime writing.

www.victorianweb.org
Authors Discussed in the Victorian Web

Overall rating: ★ ★ ★ ★			
Classification:	Webring	**Readability:**	★ ★ ★ ★
Updating:	Unclear	**Content:**	★ ★ ★ ★ ★
Navigation:	★ ★ ★ ★	**Speed:**	★ ★ ★ ★

US

This page is part of the excellent Victorian Web, an academic webring run by George P. Landow, the Professor of English and Art History at Brown University. Click on one of the entries in this simple directory to visit the author's homepage on the Victorian Web. Each homepage forms the gateway to a network of links to discussion papers by academics on particular aspects of the author's work. The homepages follow one of two simple formats; either a set of bright blue boxes labelled with a theme which leads to a list of links to relevant articles or a page of links carefully categorised under headings. Homepages for a handful of pre-Victorian writers, including Jane Austen and William Wordsworth, are also accessible. This site is a particularly useful resource for students studying the literature of the period, from the writing of John Stuart Mill to the novels of Wilkie Collins.

Part of the excellent Victorian Web, this site taps into a wide range of links to academic papers on nineteenth century authors.

OTHER SITES OF INTEREST

About.com: Women Writers
http://womenwriters.about.com

Part of the American About.com network, this site offers features and links to a mine of information on women writers from around the internet. The homepage has hyperlinks to a few articles held on the site, but the best of what's available is to be found through the left-hand Subjects index which ranges from Feminist to Sci-Fi/Fantasy and includes American, British and Canadian Writers, Self-Help, Food and Poetry. Each subject has its own homepage with an annotated list of links to choose from, including a set of Sponsored Links which usually involve commercial sites rather than sources of information. Look beneath the subject index on the homepage for links to other relevant About.com sites. Despite its obvious commercial slant, this site is well worth a visit.

BBC Books: by Author
www.bbc.co.uk/arts/books/author/

Part of the BBC's *Bookcase* magazine, this web page offers a directory of biographical essays on authors, ranging from Chinua Achebe to Joanna Trollope, which are sometimes accompanied by links to other websites.

Bloomsbury: Authors
www.bloomsbury.com/authors
Along with several other publishers, Bloomsbury have created a set of homepages for many of its authors, including J K Rowling, Joanna Trollope and Will Self, at its website. Homepages include an author biography, a list of the author's books plus a set of links to other material such as audio extracts and readers' guides at the top of the page. Well researched links to external sites can be found at the bottom of the page together with a link to the Bloomsbury Authors Diary. Some entries for more obscure authors are a little thin in content.

Fireandwater.com: Authors
www.fireandwater.com/authors
As part of its wide-ranging Fire and Water website HarperCollins has set an Authors homepage from which you can access individual author homepages, interviews and a selection of special feature sites for particular authors such as Carol Shields, although some of these are simple promotional pages created to coincide with the publication of a particular book. Author homepages include biographical details, a list of the author's books together with links to related features on the site and the author's own website where appropriate.

Chapter 03

publishers' sites and trade news

publishers

Although some publishers still design their sites simply as an online catalogue, many have begun to use them in a much more creative way, offering an abundance of magazine-style articles, interviews and book extracts at attractive looking sites which are a pleasure to browse. Some outstanding sites are paving the way and providing exciting online communities for their customers. A good example is Lonely Planet, whose notice boards provide an excellent chance to exchange information on more out of the way destinations with other seasoned travellers. Independent publisher Canongate's also has a lively and entertaining site.

Sites in this section appear in alphabetical order.

bloomsbury

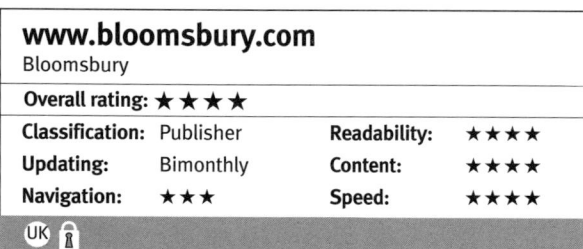

www.bloomsbury.com
Bloomsbury

Overall rating: ★ ★ ★ ★		
Classification: Publisher	**Readability:**	★ ★ ★ ★
Updating: Bimonthly	**Content:**	★ ★ ★ ★
Navigation: ★ ★ ★	**Speed:**	★ ★ ★ ★

UK

The smart homepage of Bloomsbury's website with its colourful icons leads to a selection of features including book extracts, a bookshop with links to Amazon.co.uk, and, of course, a Harry Potter section. Once in the site, it's well worth visiting the site map for an overview of what's on offer as there's lots to explore but navigation can be tricky in some areas. Features include a comprehensive calendar of literary events, information on Bloomsbury authors and competitions, while News and Gossip picks up on literary debates in the press and On This Day celebrates an event in literary history. You will need to register to buy one of Bloomsbury's literary courses (see below), to post at any of the site's notice boards or to join the Bloomsbury Reading Club, but registration is both easy and free. Although the site can be a little slow to load, response is reasonably fast.

SPECIAL FEATURES

Research Centre offers online access to Bloomsbury's reference database which includes a dictionary of quotations and an encyclopedia.

Children's Books Following the phenomenal success of the Harry Potter series, Bloomsbury have expanded their range of children's books and this is reflected in their colourful children's homepage. Lots of features to choose from including author interviews although, sadly, not with J K Rowling, listings of author events and a Book of the Month. Visit Fun Stuff for e-cards, screensavers and competitions.

Courses are on offer in the Bookshop section. Aimed at providing a grounding in critical reading, courses range from Magic Realism in Latin American literature to First World War poetry. Click on Read More to display a detailed description of the course including the tutor's CV, a book list and a prospectus outlining the modules that make up the course. To get a flavour of the course contents, click on Preview beneath the icon next to the course title. Courses are designed to be taken at your own pace.

Bloomsbury's smart website offers a variety of features including literary courses, a reference database and, of course, the latest news on Harry Potter.

canongate books

www.canongate.net			
Canongate Books			
Overall rating: ★ ★ ★ ★ ★			
Classification: Publisher		**Readability:**	★ ★ ★ ★
Updating: Monthly		**Content:**	★ ★ ★ ★ ★
Navigation: ★ ★ ★ ★		**Speed:**	★ ★ ★ ★
UK 🔒			

Canongate is one of the UK's most innovative independent publishers with imprints stretching from the cultish Payback Press to Pocket Canons, a collection of individual books from the Bible introduced by contemporary literary authors such as Louis de Bernieres and Will Self. Canongate's lively homepage may seem a little crowded at first glance but once the layout of features to the left, book information to the right and news in the middle, has been grasped, it's easy to find your way around. Basic features such as browsing Canongate's catalogue, signing up for free membership and the help screen, can be found at the top right of the screen. Books are offered for sale at a generous discount and can be bought securely. Members are entitled to extra offers, including a free book with every order, newsletters and other discounts. The site includes a set of links to an eclectic mix of other literary sites.

SPECIAL FEATURES

Canongate Imprints Each of Canongate's imprints has its own homepage, with an introduction to the imprint's style and content at the top. There are short articles by authors and news about awards, films and other events. Click on book titles to find out about new publications. Book descriptions are lively and reasonably free of marketing hype. Each imprint has its own discounts and offers listed on its homepage.

Canongate Events This feature lists details of marketing promotions and author tours as well as events with which Canongate has strong links, such as the Edinburgh Book Festival.

This lively site reflects the style of one of the UK's most interesting independent publishers.

dorling kindersley

www.dk.com
Dorling Kindersley

Overall rating: ★ ★ ★			
Classification: Publisher		Readability:	★ ★ ★
Updating: Unclear		Content:	★ ★ ★
Navigation: ★ ★ ★ ★		Speed:	★ ★ ★

UK 🔒

Well known for the quality of both their adult and children's reference books, Dorling Kindersley's website includes a secure book shop together with a selection of magazine-style features based on books published by DK, offering a taster so that you can try before you buy. The menu bar across the top of the screen lists what's available including sections for Arts & Culture, Science & History, Travel and Parenting. New titles are highlighted on each subject homepage together with an option to browse by particular Areas of Interest, competitions, features and the chance to register for a free email newsletter. Because the site uses a large number of graphics, loading can be slow.

SPECIAL FEATURE

Kid's Club offers games, screensavers and clip art together with competitions and special offers on books. The How a Book is Made feature, while interesting, is likely to appeal more to adults than children.

This website features lots of content based on DK's books so that you can sample before you buy.

harpercollins

www.fireandwater.co.uk
HarperCollins: Fire and Water

Overall rating: ★ ★ ★ ★			
Classification: Publisher		Readability:	★ ★ ★
Updating: Weekly		Content:	★ ★ ★
Navigation: ★ ★ ★ ★		Speed:	★ ★ ★

UK 🔒

HarperCollins' distinctively named website has much to offer in the way of news, book extracts and competitions plus an extensive database of author homepages. A weekly updated selection of new features such as author interviews is highlighted on the homepage, together with any news items. The Info & Help page is a useful first stop, covering information ranging from software requirements and downloads for listening to audio clips or watching video interviews, to details of competitions. The rest of the site is reasonably easy to navigate, if a little slow. To the right of the screen a subject menu leads to homepages which highlight new releases, suggests books to read from the publisher's backlist and offer a selection of signed copies of books. Book descriptions can include review extracts together with links to an author homepage, interview or other related features at the site. The drop down menus on the horizontal navigation bar lead to other features such as audio clips and book extracts, author homepages and an events diary, plus a selection of competitions. There are quick links to other specialist HarperCollins websites such as the mind, body and spirit imprints Thorsons and Element. Books published by HarperCollins can be bought securely at the site.

SPECIAL FEATURES

Members can sign up for a variety of newsletters ranging from the Voyager science fiction magazine to children's book news and regular notification of new competitions. They can also register with the Author Alert service to be kept up to date on chosen authors. Members receive a generous discount on a selection of books plus free postage and packing within the UK.

E-books can be found in the Perfect Bound pages which provide a catalogue plus details on the various formats available. Sample chapters can be downloaded from most of the e-books and a few come with special features such as an author interview or animation. Currently, e-books do not appear on the subject menu but can be found via New Releases the top left of the main homepage. There is a newsletter devoted to new e-book releases.

With its extensive database of author homepages, interviews and competitions HarperCollins' Fire and Water website has much to offer but delivery is a little slow.

lonely planet

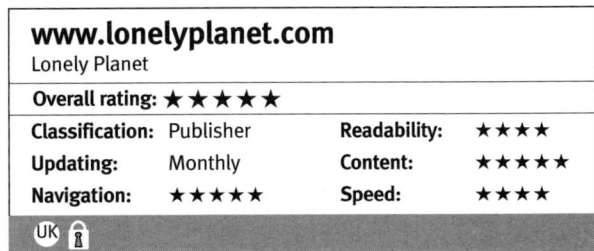

www.lonelyplanet.com			
Lonely Planet			
Overall rating: ★ ★ ★ ★			
Classification:	Publisher	**Readability:**	★ ★ ★ ★
Updating:	Monthly	**Content:**	★ ★ ★ ★ ★
Navigation:	★ ★ ★ ★ ★	**Speed:**	★ ★ ★ ★
UK 🔒			

Lonely Planet's lively website includes a weekly traveller's tales column, tips on healthy travelling and a lively travellers' community, as well as a bookshop and searchable catalogues. The homepage highlights what's new at the site while the icons to the left indicate what else is available. The site offers several newsletters including Scoop, a travel news roundup. Books can be bought securely at the site, but there are no discounts.

SPECIAL FEATURES

Traveller at Large is a lengthy weekly column based on the travels of a Lonely Planet editor, ranging from experiences of dealing with beggars in Calcutta to visiting Dubrovnik, physically restored but still bearing the scars of war. There is an archive of the columns to explore.

Theme Guides offers a solution to the dilemma of where to go by suggesting a set of themes from Art to Roadtrips. Each section lists a set of appropriate destinations with enticing descriptions, details of how to get there and links to relevant sites.

Subway is a set of categorised links to a wide variety of sites. Ranging from Destination Links, which cover tourist information, to Health and Safety guidelines and tips on ethical travelling in Issues and Reportage, this is an invaluable list for the independent traveller.

On the Road is Lonely Planet's magazine-style guide to their travel writing catalogue. The left-hand menu bar lists features contributed to On the Road by writers for the series plus all the books, categorised by country. Entries can be variable with some offering lengthy extracts while others are slightly gimmicky marketing aids.

Thorn Tree is Lonely Planet's bulletin board. Categorised by country, the board is full of requests for travel tips, many of which meet with friendly and knowledgeable replies. You don't need to register in order to post a message although registration allows you to communicate directly with other members.

Travel Ticker keeps you up to date on issues likely to affect travel plans, from health warnings to strikes, protests and public holidays. There are links to other useful advisory sites including the Foreign Office. This feature is updated monthly and archives are easily accessed.

Postcards are contributed by readers and include travelling tips plus suggestions on the best places to visit. They're not always in chronological order so it's worth checking the date if you intend to take up some of the advice offered.

This website is packed with practical advice and information.

oxford university press

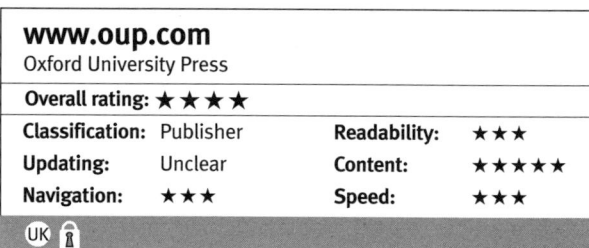

www.oup.com			
Oxford University Press			
Overall rating: ★ ★ ★ ★			
Classification: Publisher		**Readability:**	★ ★ ★
Updating: Unclear		**Content:**	★ ★ ★ ★ ★
Navigation: ★ ★ ★		**Speed:**	★ ★ ★

A glance at the large number of categories listed on the Oxford University Press main homepage will indicate the breadth of subjects covered by this publishing house. Categories include English language teaching, children's fiction and poetry plus music, law, science, medicine and the humanities to name but a few. Many of these will be of interest only to academic specialists but there is much here to interest the general reader. The homepage links a number of subsites such as the Oxford English Dictionary site, the American National Biography Online, Ask Oxford and Children's Fiction and Poetry. As a result, navigation can be unpredictable in some areas and you will find yourself resorting to your browser back button, although in general the Quick Links drop-down menu at the top of the page is the easiest way to find your way around.

SPECIAL FEATURES

Reading Room offers books extracts by subject, ranging from anthropology to sociology. Extracts are lengthy and can take some time to download. You will need Adobe Acrobat Reader to access the text which is in PDF format.

This feature can either be reached either from subject homepages or via the alphabetical site index for a full list of subject areas covered.

Oxford World's Classics has its own website which includes a magazine with quizzes, articles and extracts from the Oxford Worlds Classic series.

Although it is likely to be of interest primarily to academics, the Oxford University Press website has much to offer the general reader prepared to cope with its quirky navigation.

penguin

www.penguin.co.uk			
Penguin			
Overall rating: ★ ★ ★ ★			
Classification:	Publisher	**Readability:**	★ ★ ★ ★
Updating:	Daily	**Content:**	★ ★ ★ ★
Navigation:	★ ★ ★	**Speed:**	★ ★ ★

Penguin have adopted a lively magazine-style approach for their website's homepage, offering lots of articles, interviews and the chance to win free books. New books feature heavily and there is a Today at Penguin feature to the right of the screen showcasing an author and book of the day, together with any recent news about the company. General features such as Author Interviews, Events Diary and Free Stuff can be found via the navigation bars at the top of the screen. Other features include Penguin Authors, a set of brief biographical notes, and the Penguin Readers Group. The site can also be browsed by subject but in the main, channel content is restricted to information on new releases. Most pages are attractively colourful but can be a little slow to load. Books can be bought from the site securely but there are no discounts.

SPECIAL FEATURES

Classics The Classics channel is a site within a site devoted to the well known Penguin Classics imprint. Along with an expanding collection of essays, the site has a Classics Trivia page that will provide hours of fun for well-read quiz addicts.

Click on **Resources** to find a small set of teachers' and readers' guides plus some interesting links to other classics sites. Free registration entitles you to join in the classics discussion forum.

EPenguin is the online home of Penguin's e-books which are available in Microsoft Reader, Palm Reader and Adobe Reader formats. There's a helpful, straightforward step-by-step guide plus an option to try an e-book. The range of books available is limited but growing

Gift Selector is a nifty little feature which allows you to specify basic information about the person you're buying for then displays suggested books.

First Chapters offers a large selection of book extracts by Penguin authors, ranging from Nick Hornby to Elizabeth David.

There is much to enjoy at this attractive site.

random house

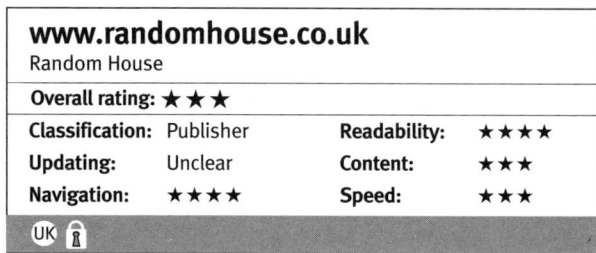

www.randomhouse.co.uk			
Random House			
Overall rating: ★ ★ ★			
Classification: Publisher		**Readability:**	★ ★ ★ ★
Updating: Unclear		**Content:**	★ ★ ★
Navigation: ★ ★ ★ ★		**Speed:**	★ ★ ★

Random House's attractive homepage highlights marketing promotions and major new titles as well as new features in its magazine pages. The navigation bar features popular sections such as Fiction or Mind, Body and Spirit while the drop-down menu can be used to focus your browsing on particular subject areas. The Poetry section has a poem to read online while children have their own brightly coloured magazine which includes games and competitions. Loading can be a little slow but it's worth the wait.

SPECIAL FEATURE

Off the Page The magazine section has lots of book excerpts from authors such as Lindsey Davis, Sebastian Faulks and Anne Tyler. Minisites is something of a mixed bag with a set of sites highlighting particular books. Content varies from a simple book description to a lengthy extract coupled with an author biography. A set of reading group guides can also be found here.

The best of Random House's website is to be found in its Off the Page magazine with lots of book extracts.

rough guides

www.roughguides.co.uk		
Rough Guides		
Overall rating: ★ ★ ★ ★		
Classification: Publisher	**Readability:**	★ ★ ★
Updating: Weekly	**Content:**	★ ★ ★ ★ ★
Navigation: ★ ★ ★	**Speed:**	★ ★ ★ ★
US		

The Rough Guides homepage is split into travel, community and music, each of which has its own homepage. Click on Travel Home then Spotlights to find weekly articles on destinations such as Turkestan, New Zealand and Kenya, with archives going back to 1998. Travel Talk offers a friendly notice board which guests can view, although if you want to contribute you will need to register, while Health offers tips for healthy travel for a variety of destinations. To return to the main homepage to visit either Music or Community you will need to click the Roughguides logo. Community is worth a visit to read members' accounts of their travels in Travel Journals. This section also hosts a travel club which offers its members travel deals but it's aimed at the American market.

SPECIAL FEATURES

Rough Guides Online   Large sections of Rough Guide travel guides can be accessed online by choosing a destination from the Countries or Featured Cities boxes at the top of the page.

Music   offers online versions of Rough Guides to World Music, Classical and Rock with lots of reviews for newly released CDs.

Visit this site to access sections of both the travel and music Rough Guides.

OTHER SITES OF INTEREST

Carcanet
www.carcanet.co.uk
One of the foremost poetry publishers in the UK, Carcanet's extensive catalogues are available to search or browse at this website. Book descriptions are thoughtful and informative with lots of cross-referencing to other entries in the catalogue. The author section features thumbnail portraits of many of Carcanet's poets ranging from Joseph Brodsky to Robert Graves. The site also features a Poem of the Day on its homepage, Poet on Poet of the Week and an Author of the Month complete with relevant links.

Fourth Estate
www.4thestate.co.uk/
Although now part of the HarperCollins empire, Fourth Estate has retained and updated it's own stylish website. The catalogue can be browsed by subject. Click on one of the book jackets to display a synopsis, reviews and links to other related material, plus details of other books by the author. Features might include articles by Fourth Estate authors, competitions or book extracts. Reading Room features a particular book complete with links, suggested

similar reading, discussion topics for reading groups, an interview and an extract. A sneak preview of future publications can be found in Coming Soon. Worth visiting for fans of Fourth Estate's distinctive catalogue which includes authors such as Dava Sobel, Carol Shields, Nigel Slater and Annie Proulx.

Granta
www.granta.com/
This site is the online home of both Granta's distinguished literary magazine and its book-publishing arm. Divided into two, one part of the website acts as a taster for the print magazine with a contents page for the latest issue including contributors' CVs plus details of all back issues, stretching back to the early eighties. Details of all Granta's authors, including any contributions they have made to the magazine, can be found in the Books section. The homepage features an interview with a Granta author and showcases new titles. Books can be bought securely at the site and it's worth looking out for special offers.

Hodder Headline
www.madaboutbooks.co.uk
Content is a little thin at Hodder Headline's Mad About Books website. There's a book of the month and a chance for sneak previews of forthcoming publications. The author lounge offers brief biographies of writers including Jake Arnott, Jean Auel and Wendy Holden with links to their homepages where available. Catalogues can be browsed by category and there is an events diary. Response can be a little slow.

Orbit Books
www.orbitbooks.co.uk
Orbit Books, the science fiction and fantasy imprint of Little, Brown, numbers Iain M. Banks, Tad Williams, and Greg Bear amongst the many authors it publishes. The main attractions of the Orbit website can be found in iAuthors which houses interviews with authors Robert Jordan and Terry Brooks. There are links to author sites plus several other science fiction and fantasy sites. The News Releases includes a list of forthcoming titles together with details of author tours. The homepage offers a free newsletter and highlights the site's book of the month which can be bought securely at the site.

Pan Macmillan
www.panmacmillan.co.uk
The usual extracts, author interviews and book synopses are available at this attractive site but content is a little thin with very short features. Author links tend to be to promotional microsites for particular books. Catalogue listings for imprints, such as Picador, Channel 4 Books and Macmillan Children's, can be browsed by subject and there are links to bookshops if you want to buy the books online. Best visit the Site Map from the Browse navigation button to see all that's available at the site. The Games section is worth a visit and there is a small selection of reading guides for book clubs.

Thames & Hudson
www.thamesandhudson.com
The catalogues of one of Britain's best known publishers of books on art, architecture and design, including the World of Art series, can be browsed online at this site, although book descriptions are minimal. Books can be bought

securely via the site and the heftily discounted monthly Special Offers are worth exploring. The Free Resources section has a useful set of links to major galleries throughout the world. This section also houses the site's most interesting feature, the beautiful woodcut illustrations from the 15th century allegorical romance, *Hypnerotomachia Poliphili,* which can be enlarged and printed.

Books at Transworld
www.booksattransworld.co.uk

This attractive new website, from the publishers of Joanne Harris, Terry Pratchett and Bill Bryson, showcases new books by subject and offers author interviews, book extracts, competitions and a diary of author events in its Put Your Feet Up magazine section. The Expert Gardening focuses on the popular Expert Gardener series with a monthly set of seasonal gardening hints taken from the series while books on the Eden Project get their own page.

Virago
www.virago.co.uk/

There's much to explore at Virago's website although perhaps not quite as much as might first be apparent as several features crop up under different headings. Choose News to find out about author events and new books, which can be bought securely through the site. The Virago section offers a history of the pioneering feminist imprint plus a set of links to websites such as The Women's Review of Books and sites for Virago authors such as Polly Samson, Antonia White and Maya Angelou. There's a small selection of reading group guides, features on Virago authors in Meet and a chance to win books in Virago's monthly competitions.

book trade news

www.thebookseller.com
The Bookseller

Overall rating: ★ ★ ★ ★			
Classification:	Trade Magazine	**Readability:**	★ ★ ★ ★
Updating:	Daily	**Content:**	★ ★ ★ ★ ★
Navigation:	★ ★ ★ ★ ★	**Speed:**	★ ★ ★

UK

The Bookseller's website is the most comprehensive online source of UK book trade news available online. Updated on a daily basis, the homepage features tasters for news stories, which can be viewed in full in the News section, and other features plus the top 40 bestselling books in the UK. Although some of the site's content is likely to be of interest only to librarians, booksellers and publishers, those with more than a passing interest in the book trade should find something to interest them here. *The Bookseller*'s publications, such as *The Books Sales Yearbook*, are available at a discount if purchased online. The site is straightforward and easily navigable. Although some areas are closed to non-subscribers, much of the site can be browsed for free.

SPECIAL FEATURES

The Book Blog Reached via News, this section has summaries of and links to book-related news and comment in the media, from the *Guardian* to the *New York Times*.

Books in the Media lists book-related TV and radio programmes for the current week, from review programmes to films based on books.

Careers Focus includes not only classified job advertisements but also links to specialist recruitment consultants and information gleaned from the book trade's annual salary survey.

Crossword for those who enjoy a literary challenge.

Interview reached from News this is a database of articles stretching back to 1995, including an extensive collection of author interviews which have appeared in the magazine. The database can only be searched by Premium members who must pay a subscription.

A handy fallback for those who never manage to get their hands on the staff room copy, The Bookseller's website provides an excellent resource for in-depth information on the UK book trade.

www.publishingnews.co.uk			
Publishing News			
Overall rating: ★ ★ ★ ★			
Classification: Trade Magazine		**Readability:**	★ ★ ★ ★
Updating: Weekly		**Content:**	★ ★ ★ ★
Navigation: ★ ★ ★ ★ ★		**Speed:**	★ ★ ★ ★
(UK)			

The online edition of *Publishing News,* the UK publishing world's trade paper, is published at this site every Friday. Trade news, gossip, bestseller charts and career opportunities in publishing can all be found with ease at this simple site. The homepage features the latest trade news headlines with more background available in the News section and there's lots of matey gossip about launch parties and trade fairs in the People pages. Registration at the site is free and opens up more services as a visit to PN membership will show.

SPECIAL FEATURE

Links for other sites include links to **literary agents, libraries** and **bookshops**. The list of publishers' links is particularly useful as it covers many small publishers in addition to the more obvious names.

This UK publishing trade paper site will interest anyone looking for an insider's view of the book world.

www.publishersweekly.com
Publishers Weekly

Overall rating: ★ ★ ★ ★			
Classification:	Trade Magazine	**Readability:**	★ ★ ★
Updating:	Daily	**Content:**	★ ★ ★ ★
Navigation:	★ ★ ★ ★	**Speed:**	★ ★ ★

US

Publishers Weekly is the premier trade paper for the American publishing industry. The online edition is crammed with information, some of which may be of interest to book lovers as well as book trade professionals. Daily trade news bulletins appear on the homepage, together with features such as roundups of forthcoming titles while chatty interviews with authors, publishers and editors can be found in the People section. Although the site is easily navigable, some of the categories such as Feature and Forecasts seem to overlap in the nature of their content. Free subscription entitles members to a daily newsletter plus access to an author's events diary but payment is required to search the archives.

SPECIAL FEATURES

ePublishing has news stories on this rapidly developing area of publishing.

Children's has a wide range of articles on children's book publishing in the US plus some international stories.

America's leading book trade journal online.

OTHER SITES OF INTEREST

book2book
www.booktrade.info
Run by a small group of publishers, booksellers and trade journalists this site aims to provide a portal for the UK book trade. The homepage features news stories in brief and also acts as navigator for the rest of the site. On offer is a detailed set of links to news stories, a range of trade directories for publishers, press and literary agents, links to book reviews, online bookshops and bestseller lists plus a set of miscellaneous links in Useful Pages which includes news agencies and the BBC UK weather forecast. Notes and Queries offers answers to questions about the book trade. Content at the site is currently a little thin but it looks promising.

Bookwire
www.bookwire.com
Bookwire acts as a gateway to American book trade resources, offering access to a wide range of trade services such as bestseller lists, a calendar of events, book trade statistics and American books-in-print listings. Although much of the site's content is likely to be of interest only to those involved in the book trade, it does offer lots of links to booksellers, publishers, libraries and other resources including book awards and book-related newsgroups.

literary magazines and newspapers online

ezines

Literary ezines abound on the internet. From one-person operations run as a hobby to the kind of well-organised, articulate and witty publication that gives even the best broadsheet arts reviews a run for their money, there's a wide variety to choose from. Links at sites run by enthusiasts are well worth a look as they often lead to other out of the way but interesting ezines. Although most of the sites reviewed in this section are run for profit, a few are simply the product of a vibrant enthusiasm with little or no monetary reward, so if you like what you see, don't feel shy about letting them know.

www.aldaily.com
Arts & Letters Daily

Overall rating: ★ ★ ★ ★ ★			
Classification: Portal		**Readability:**	★ ★ ★
Updating: Daily		**Content:**	★ ★ ★ ★ ★
Navigation: ★ ★ ★ ★		**Speed:**	★ ★ ★ ★

(US)

Don't be put off by the sheer density of information presented on the homepage of this literary digest. Its declared aim is to draw together the most intelligent, articulate and illuminating articles published on the internet and it's largely successful in achieving it. A glance at the masthead at the top of the screen indicates that the site covers much more than just books, ranging from links to articles on philosophy and aesthetics to disputes and gossip. Although it may appear daunting at first, navigation is relatively easy once it becomes clear that the screen has four basic components: a categorised list of links to other sites to the left of the screen, together with three columns headed Articles of Note, New Books, and Essays and Opinion. Each of the three columns is made up of a series of brief introductions to articles, followed by a link to the site at which it is published. A certain amount of guess work may be required if you're looking for something in particular as, for instance, book titles are not mentioned in links to reviews. There is no keyword search facility at the site and perhaps the best way to approach it is as if you were browsing the contents page of an international broadsheet newspaper. New entries appear at the top of the relevant column and remain on the site for an average of two or three days before they are added to the yearly archives. It's certainly worth bookmarking any article that catches your eye as, with no keyword search, patience is needed for browsing the archives, which stretch back to 1998. The site reflects the truly international nature of the internet with a registered office in Washington DC, an editor in New Zealand and links to English-speaking sites throughout the world.

SPECIAL FEATURES
Along the left-hand side of the screen runs a list of links that lead you straight to a variety of information media, ranging from national newspaper websites such as *The Australian*, *Boston Globe* and the *Jerusalem Post*, to a set of search engines. Some of the more notable sets of links are listed below.

Breaking News includes Reuters, CNN and the BBC

Magazines is an extensive list of links to a wide range of periodicals including *The Economist, Prospect*, *The New Yorker* and *New Scientist*.

Columnists links to the archives of a variety of websites for collections of articles by a wide range of columnists including Alistair Cooke and Robert Fisk.

Book Reviews leads straight to the books pages of a variety of sites, from *Salon*, one of the internet's most interesting arts commentators to the *Telegraph*.

Favouties links to ezines covering all manner of subjects, from *Killing the Buddha*, a non-sectarian religious magazine, to the eccentric *Obscure Store*, which specialises in weird and wonderful news stories.

Radio News tunes into news stations around the world, from the BBC World Service to Australia ABC. You will need Realplayer software to take advantage of these links. If you don't already have it, scroll down to the bottom right of this site's homepage for simple instructions on how to download it. A small selection of jazz and classical music stations is also available at *Arts & Daily*, further down the page.

Diversions offers links to a little diversion, from *Dilbert* to the sharply satirical *Onion* ezine.

Perfect for those who love to trawl the Sunday broadsheets, this daily literary digest is packed with the best writing the internet has to offer on the arts and much more besides.

www.janmag.com
January Magazine

Overall rating: ★ ★ ★ ★ ★			
Classification:	Ezine	**Readability:**	★ ★ ★ ★
Updating:	Daily	**Content:**	★ ★ ★ ★ ★
Navigation:	★ ★ ★ ★ ★	**Speed:**	★ ★ ★ ★

US

This uncomplicated, no-frills American magazine can come as something of a relief after the all-singing, all-dancing literary sites that try to cover everything. *January Magazine* concentrates on providing reviews for recently released books across a range of categories, from fiction to cook books, plus a set of informative author profiles and features such as book excerpts or roundups of favourite books. Contributors range from the likes of Tom Wolfe to reviewers who may not be very well known, but who deliver competent, well-expressed reviews. New additions to the site are featured on its homepage and a simple key word search will produce relevant entries from the archives. Subscription to regular updates at the site is both free and simple and navigation couldn't be easier. Click on Music to view January's sister music magazine site, *Blue Coupe*.

SPECIAL FEATURES

Crime Fiction is particularly well catered for, with a separate newsletter and a set of links to interesting crime writing sites.

A simple, fresh-looking site which concentrates on delivering articulate reviews as well as features and author interviews.

www.richmondreview.co.uk
The Richmond Review

Overall rating: ★ ★ ★ ★			
Classification:	Ezine	**Readability:**	★ ★ ★ ★ ★
Updating:	Monthly	**Content:**	★ ★ ★ ★
Navigation:	★ ★ ★ ★ ★	**Speed:**	★ ★ ★ ★ ★

UK

One of the UK's first online literary magazines, *The Richmond Review* has gained a reputation for the quality of its writing. The emphasis is firmly on the literary, with a few nods to American cult crime writers and the occasional foray into other areas of the arts. Reviews, articles and interviews are intelligent, witty and well-informed written in a tone that reflects the obvious passion of its contributors for modern writing. Poetry is given a high profile with its own section on the Reviews page. Many of *The Richmond Review*'s editors and contributors work in the London publishing world, but the friendly Who We Are page offers the assurance that they are not allowed to review books published by the companies they work for. The homepage showcases new contributions together with a set of recent articles and reviews. Archived reviews and features can be found via the simple navigation bar which appears at the top and bottom of the page. The magazine forms part of a small network and there are links to *Spike*, *Crime Time*, *book2book* and the film magazine, *kamera.co.uk*.

SPECIAL FEATURES

The Library houses a selection of short stories, essays and poetry, ranging from curiosities such as Salman Rushdie's *Commencement Address at Bard College* in 1996, to Tibor Fischer's short story, *Bookcruncher*. Links to author pages and other related websites appear alongside each entry, together with merchandise links to the author's books at amazon.co.uk or Barnes and Noble.

Features Quick Chat interviews with authors such as Iain M. Banks and American cult crime writer, Eddie Bunker, head the index of features in this area of the site. Other articles range from an extract from Darcey Bussell's account of her experiences as a ballet dancer to Demon Dog Central, *The Richmond Review*'s homage to one of their heroes, the crime writer, James Ellroy. Essays tackle serious subjects and are well argued and articulate. Contributions from authors such as Julia O'Faolain and Russell Celyn Jones seem to be on the increase.

The stylish writing at this literary site rivals the best of the Sunday paper arts review sections.

www.salon.com/books
Salon.com

Overall rating: ★ ★ ★ ★ ★			
Classification:	Ezine	**Readability:**	★ ★ ★ ★
Updating:	Daily	**Content:**	★ ★ ★ ★ ★
Navigation:	★ ★ ★ ★ ★	**Speed:**	★ ★ ★ ★

US £

The American ezine, *Salon* has carved-out a reputation for itself as one of the sharpest arts and current affairs magazines on the internet and its books pages certainly live up to expectations. Although much of the content is now only available by paying a subscription, it can be viewed via a free seven-day trial subscription which offers a taster of all that's available. You need to be aware that you will have to give your credit card number for this and that if you do not cancel at the end of your seven-day period an annual subscription fee will be billed. The subscription rate is reasonable and you can opt to pay more for Salon Premium, the advertisement-free channel. The Books homepage highlights recent articles, interviews and reviews. Visit Directory at the top of the left-hand bar for a full and detailed listing of what's currently available throughout the magazine. Book Reviews, under Hot Topics on the left-hand menu bar leads not only to the current reviews but also to a fully searchable archive. Scroll down to Particpate for a link to TableTalk, Salon's discussion forums, and to specific topics in other areas of the main site. The site is reasonably easy to navigate but if you should find yourself lost, the Books homepage can always be found via the bar at the top of the page. *Salon*'s archives are easily accessible and can be searched alphabetically by subject, by clicking on either

All of Salon.com or By Department under the Articles by Date heading beneath the Hot Topics listing. There's also a quick search box at the top right of the screen.

SPECIAL FEATURES

Book Bag can be found under Hot Topics on the left-hand bar, and leads to an eclectic set of book recommendations on particular themes from authors such as Rick Moody, Jane Hamilton and John Franzen.

Dear Mr Blue Sadly, Garrison Keillor has now relinquished his Dear Mr Blue column after a serious heart operation but fans can still find his work in the archives.

Audio has its own homepage. Lots of audiobooks excerpts to be played from this section and a visit to Audio How-To via the link at the bottom of any audio page will solve any problems you might have in listening to audio clips. Special Audio Features, to the right, changes frequently and ranges from rare recordings, such as Ernest Hemingway reading his short story *In Harry's Bar in Venice*, to audio clips of author interviews. It also includes links to other audio sites of interest. There is a wide range of new audiobook reviews with a facility to browse by genre from the left-hand navigation bar. This section of Salon.com offers a welcome focus on an area of publishing frequently overlooked by other magazines.

Salon's Books pages offer a lively commentary on literary life, including particularly detailed and varied coverage of audio books.

www.bbc.co.uk/arts/books
BBC Books

Overall rating: ★ ★ ★ ★			
Classification:	Ezine	**Readability:**	★ ★ ★ ★
Updating:	Bimonthly	**Content:**	★ ★ ★ ★
Navigation:	★ ★ ★ ★	**Speed:**	★ ★ ★ ★

UK

http://jacketmagazine.com
Jacket

Overall rating: ★ ★ ★ ★			
Classification:	Ezine	**Readability:**	★ ★ ★ ★
Updating:	Thrice Yearly	**Content:**	★ ★ ★ ★ ★
Navigation:	★ ★ ★	**Speed:**	★ ★ ★ ★

AU

There's much to explore in the BBC's book magazine although you'll need to look out for links to the right of the screen as well as the menu to the left. The main homepage lists new features while poetry, crime, science fiction, romance, children's books and women's writing all have their own homepages with features such as advice on writing for the genre or author interviews. Authors A–Z is well worth visiting for biographical essays on authors ranging from Chinua Achebe to Joanna Trollope. You'll have to register to use the message boards but they're lively and well frequented. Articles in Book News are often chatty, informative and entertaining although sometimes a little too general to be designated as 'news'.

SPECIAL FEATURES

Poetry is particularly well served with a separate homepage in the BBC Arts section to which the Books section is linked. Features include a resident poet, the Poetry Corner message board plus a selection of poetry readings by poets ranging from Ted Hughes to Benjamin Zephaniah.

Both entertaining and informative, the BBC's book magazine offers many interesting features, particularly for poetry fans.

Although this site might look slightly amateurish at first glance, the respect it has earned from journals such as *Time* magazine is well deserved. Set up by Australian poet John Tranter in October 1997, *Jacket* showcases new poetry and includes literary essays, interviews and reviews. All issues can be searched by key word or browsed, either from the Catalog, through the link on the homepage, or by selecting an issue number from the top of the screen. The site is based around a simple homepage but the many links require some patience to navigate. New issues can be browsed as they are constructed.

SPECIAL FEATURES

Literary Links is best reached from the bottom of the Jacket Catalog or About Jacket page and is well worth a visit for those interested in similar small literary magazines. The page also includes a link to a directory of Australian literature sites at the top of the screen. Further examples of John Tranter's own writing can be found through a link in the section about himself, about halfway down the homepage.

Well worth a visit for poetry fans, this site also hosts a set of interesting links to other magazines.

www.spikemagazine.com
Spike Magazine

Overall rating: ★ ★ ★ ★			
Classification:	Ezine	Readability:	★ ★ ★ ★
Updating:	Unclear	Content:	★ ★ ★ ★
Navigation:	★ ★ ★ ★	Speed:	★ ★ ★ ★

UK

Spike is an eclectic UK magazine run by Chris Mitchell, for fun rather than profit. *Spike*'s writing is often stylish and articulate ranging from reflections on the Coen brothers' films to articles on Derek Jarman and interviews with the likes of A. L. Kennedy, William Gibson and Jeff Noon. Book reviews are not confined to new titles but might include books by William S. Burroughs or Saul Bellow. Updating of the site is described as 'erratic' by Chris, but new features are highlighted on the homepage. Navigation is clear, apart from returning to the homepage which needs a click on the *Spike* logo. *Spike* also includes music reviews.

SPECIAL FEATURES

Splinters is a pleasing mishmash of observations on anything from TV documentaries to literary birthdays, accompanied by an appropriate set of links.

Links includes well-researched pages on Spike favourites, Will Self, Jeff Noon, J. G. Ballard and Irvine Welsh plus links to the pick of reviews, interviews and articles.

An eclectic magazine that will please fans of Will Self, Irvine Welsh and J.G. Ballard.

newspapers and magazines online

Some magazines and newspapers such as *The Guardian* and America's *Atlantic Monthly* have managed the transition from print to screen with creative skill and enthusiasm, designing sites far richer in content than the original print versions. Others appear less keen and simply transfer their editorial content from print to screen with little or no additions. Whichever is the case, most still generously offer free online access and how else would you get to browse the books pages of *The New York Times* over your morning coffee unless you have the services of a particularly cosmopolitan newsagent?

www.theatlantic.com
The Atlantic Online

Overall rating: ★ ★ ★ ★ ★			
Classification:	Magazine	Readability:	★ ★ ★ ★
Updating:	Weekly	Content:	★ ★ ★ ★ ★
Navigation:	★ ★ ★ ★ ★	Speed:	★ ★ ★ ★

US

Founded in 1857, *The Atlantic Monthly* is one of the USA's most venerable journals, covering a wide range of topics from culture and politics, to food and travel. *The Atlantic*'s website is made up of three sections: *Atlantic Unbound*, the online journal which focuses on books, literature and culture; In the Magazine, which contains a selection of articles from the current print magazine; and From the Archives, a dip into *The Atlantic*'s extensive archive. Each section appears on every page, but the sections are colour-coded, easing navigation around this meaty site. The pages most likely to interest book lovers, Books & Critics, Poetry Pages and Fiction, which showcases original short stories, are all easily found from the left-hand navigation bar. Each piece of writing has links to related items, both at *The Atlantic* site and elsewhere. Registration is required for Transatlantic, the free weekly newsletter. The quality of writing at this site is all that you would expect from a journal that has become a cultural institution in the United States with debates at the Post & Riposte reader forum matching the wide-ranging and articulate debates in the magazines

SPECIAL FEATURES

From the Archives All issues of the online journal, *Atlantic Unbound*, are archived, together with selected articles from the print magazine stretching back to its inception. From the Archives presents highlights on each category homepage, ranging from an essay on journalism and morality from the June 1926 issue of *The Atlantic Monthly*, to a review of Walt Whitman's *Leaves of Grass*, dated January 1882. The archive homepage, reached from the left-hand navigation bar, features a useful set of topic indexes, including a small section on classic book reviews. You will now be charged a small fee to search and freely access the archives but the richness of their content makes it well worth it.

Poetry Pages this section of *The Atlantic Unbound* is particularly rich in content, with reviews, interviews, essays and appreciations. The In the Magazine section feature poems commissioned for *The Atlantic*, alongside work from established and classic poets. Poems labelled Soundings

have audio clips, although sound quality can vary. You'll need Real Player software if you want to listen to these and there's help available if you need to download it.

Fiction Short stories commissioned by *The Atlantic* can be found on the Fiction pages, alongside selections from the archive which might include work by John Updike, Vladimir Nabokov or Louisa May Alcott.

Post & Riposte *The Atlantic Unbound*'s discussion area can be reached via Forum on the left-hand navigation bar. Conference areas are ranged by subject, although registration entitles you to post messages in any area. Debates are lively, informed and articulate with occasional lapses into frivolity or name-calling, roundly castigated. Registration is free and personal details can be included when registering. Both these and email addresses are displayed by clicking on the name of the contributor but this facility is restricted to fellow members.

The online home of a venerable American literary institution, this site is both a rich source of cultural history and contemporary literary debate.

www.guardianunlimited.co.uk/books

Guardian Unlimited: Books

Overall rating: ★ ★ ★ ★ ★			
Classification:	Newspaper	Readability:	★ ★ ★ ★
Updating:	Daily	Content:	★ ★ ★ ★ ★
Navigation:	★ ★ ★ ★	Speed:	★ ★ ★

UK

Visitors to the *Guardian Unlimited* books pages might find themselves uttering that hoary old chestnut so often heard in the best bookshops, 'I could stay here all day'. There's certainly enough to keep you occupied with articles and reviews gathered from the pages of the *Guardian* and the *Observer*, literary games, book extracts, discussion boards plus a well-chosen set of links to other literary sites, if you still haven't had enough. As with all large websites, a visit to the Help page is advisable for first-timers and you may find that this becomes a regular navigation point, as some of the features listed here, such as Adrian Mole's Diary, can be difficult to track down elsewhere. The homepage highlights book news with pointers to other features to the left and right of the screen. To visit the basic elements of the site, click the appropriate link on the navigation bar across the top of the screen. Click By Genre to browse content for areas of special interest, Extracts for book extracts together with relevant links, and Authors for a database of well over 100 author biographies. Throughout the site there are links to amazon.co.uk and readers should visit What to Buy for the *Guardian*'s pick of the best recently published books. Speed can undoubtedly be a problem with this site, but the reward for patience is an unrivalled source of information and critical literary debate.

SPECIAL FEATURES

Top 10s An eclectic mix of personalities, including Mohamed Al Fayed, Malcolm McClaren and Anthony Bourdain, choose ten books that have caught their eye on a particular theme.

Games Have fun with Poetry Moodmatcher which will try and match a poem to what ever outlandish answers you care to enter in its selection criteria, or try one of the taxing literary quizzes on a variety of subjects from Harry Potter to feminist literature. Parts of this section can be very slow, particularly when checking quiz results.

LRB Essay *Guardian Unlimited* hosts the *London Review of Books'* weekly essay on subjects ranging from theology to the Holocaust. An archive of essays can also be found in this section and there is a reciprocal link with the LRB website.

Talk is the way into *Guardian Unlimited*'s literary discussion boards. You will need to register and log in to take part but discussions can be browsed to gain a flavour of their content. Subjects range from book buying habits to What Are You Reading Today? The tone is chatty but informed with lots of regular contributors, lending a nice community feel to the forums. *Guardian Unlimited*'s Reading Group can be found in this section.

Guardian Unlimited offers the most comprehensive coverage of book news, reviews and features of any online UK newspaper or magazine, although a degree of patience is required to retrieve some of the information on offer.

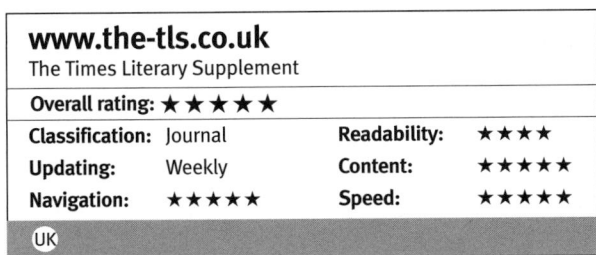

www.the-tls.co.uk
The Times Literary Supplement

Overall rating: ★ ★ ★ ★			
Classification:	Journal	**Readability:**	★ ★ ★ ★
Updating:	Weekly	**Content:**	★ ★ ★ ★ ★
Navigation:	★ ★ ★ ★ ★	**Speed:**	★ ★ ★ ★ ★

UK

The online website of the UK's most distinguished literary journal acts both as a taster for the print edition, and a gateway to the *Times Literary Supplement*'s magnificent Centenary Archive. Many features are available only to paid-up subscribers to the print journal but there is much to sample before signing up, including short versions of several reviews from the current week's edition, highlights of recent reviews by subject and a sneak preview of what's available in the Centenary Archives. The **About the TLS** pages offer a flavour of the journal with a brief history of its content and an impressive list of past and present contributors, ranging from T. S. Eliot to Seamus Heaney. A free weekly email newsletter is available from the homepage, via Book Listings.

SPECIAL FEATURES

TLS Subscriber Archive Free to print edition subscribers, the TLS archives stretch back to 1994.

TLS Centenary Archives requires a separate subscription. These archives contain all issues of the TLS dating from its inception in 1902. Click on the free trial option on the Centenary Archive page to view an introduction to the archives and try some sample searches. Libraries may register for further free trials.

A taster for the print edition of the Times Literary Supplement, this website also offers access to the splendours of the TLS's Centenary Archive for those who wish to subscribe to it.

www.nytimes.com/pages/books
The New York Times

Overall rating: ★ ★ ★ ★			
Classification: Newspaper		**Readability:**	★ ★ ★ ★
Updating: Daily		**Content:**	★ ★ ★ ★ ★
Navigation: ★ ★ ★		**Speed:**	★ ★ ★ ★

(US)

The books section of *The New York Times* offers up to the minute American book news and lengthy and intelligent reviews by authors such as Jay McInerney. Although there is a navigation bar to the left of the screen, it's best to browse the homepage to see what's available as not all book-related features appear on the bar. Archives can be searched for reviews and articles going back to 1996. You'll need to register to get beyond the site's homepage. Registration is both free and secure although you will be asked to give information about your circumstances.

SPECIAL FEATURES

Readers' Opinions are on the left-hand navigation bar under Opinion. The books section hosts a reading group as part of *The New York Times* on the Web Forums but you will find a variety of other literary topics under discussion. Discussions are thoughtful and intelligent but occasionally rather waspish. Archived discussions are available.

Sunday Book Review The complete Sunday Book Review can be accessed online including extensive book reviews, author interviews, editors' choice and bestsellers. Archives for the Sunday Book Review stretch back to 1997.

Audio This section houses a fascinating selection of audio clips including poetry readings by W.H. Auden and Sylvia Plath. You'll need Real Player software, easily downloadable via a link at the site, to listen to these.

First Chapters There are literally hundreds of first chapters available at the site, including many by British writers.

Home to some of America's sharpest literary commentators.

www.Sunday-times.co.uk
The Sunday Times

Overall rating: ★ ★ ★ ★			
Classification: Newspaper		**Readability:**	★ ★ ★ ★
Updating: Weekly		**Content:**	★ ★ ★ ★
Navigation: ★ ★ ★ ★		**Speed:**	★ ★ ★ ★ ★

UK R

This straightforward site offers the same intelligent and informed book coverage which appears in the print edition of the *Sunday Times*. The simple homepage lists the features available including reviews of major new books, children's books, audio books, a short selection of crucial reads in You Really Must Read, a brief diary of literary events on offer for the week in Book Events and a little literary gossip in Diary. You will need to register with the site to access its features. Registration is both simple and free but do remember to untick the relevant boxes if you want to avoid unwanted emails. Reviewed books can be bought securely and at a discount from Times Books Direct although links from the Book Circle section of the site may take you to another online bookshop such as W H Smith.

SPECIAL FEATURES

Book Circle features Q & A sessions with a wide range of authors from Philip Pullman to Matthew Kneale.

In the News features a useful list of books with which to catch up with the background behind the weeks headlines.

A Little Night Reading An author writes about their current choice of reading.

The online edition of The Sunday Times books pages.

OTHER SITES OF INTEREST

The Independent: Books
http://enjoyment.independent.co.uk/books/
Boyd Tonkin's often acerbic, wide-ranging Week in Books column is the highlight of the *Independent*'s online books pages and there are plenty of archived columns to enjoy. Other features including book news stories and author interviews. There's lots of thoughtful review coverage culled from the newspaper's pages, and the site includes a drop down menu of the most recent book reviews to help you track down exactly what you're after. Unfortunately, text is confined to one column which takes up just over a third of the screen resulting in lots of scrolling while reading reviews.

The Telegraph: Books
www.telegraph.co.uk
The homepage of the *Telegraph*'s online literary section includes links to full reviews of important new books plus a paperback roundup together with regular diary and literary gossip columns. Reviews are informed and intelligent with contributions from writers such as Patrick Gale, A N Wilson and Barbara Trapido. You will need to register with the site to access its features. Registration is both simple and free but do remember to tick the relevant box if you want to avoid

unwanted emails. Books can be bought online via a direct link to amazon.co.uk.

London Review of Books
www.lrb.co.uk

Set up in 1979, the *London Review of Books* is a serious literary magazine which attracts contributions from a wide range of distinguished writers, critics and commentators. Designed to act as a taster for the print magazine, the LRB site showcases several essays from its current edition together with the contents page and a selection of letters. Subscribers can explore the archives by subject and contributor or by keywords through the search facility. A discount is offered on print edition subscriptions which are submitted online.

Crime Time
www.Crimetime.co.uk

Attached to the UK print magazine of the same name, the *Crime Time* site features reviews, interviews, features and profiles often written in an entertainingly opinionated style. New features appear at the top of the homepage, with pointers to recent contributions further down. Click on Reviews for an A–Z listing while Features lists articles on particular aspects of crime writing, movies and TV crime programmes. The Interviews section includes chats with Caleb Carr, Michael Dibdin and James Ellroy, and there is a small selection of author profiles.

The Age
http://theage.com.au/entertainment/books/index.html

The online edition of one of Australia's national newspapers, *The Age* carries book reviews together with a wide range of thoughtful full-length features. Archives can be searched for a small fee.

children and young adults

advice and recommendations

Most parents and many teachers are eager for advice when it to comes to choosing books for children. The sheer quantity of titles available can seem a bit daunting, with children's bookshop sections mirroring the subject areas covered by books for adults. Then there's the question of the right book for the right age group. The internet comes to the rescue here with sites set up specifically to offer advice and recommendations from children's book specialists, together with recommendations of favourites by children and young adults which should help engage the interest of more reluctant readers.

www.achuka.co.uk/index.html

Achuka

Overall rating: ★ ★ ★ ★ ★			
Classification:	Ezine	Readability:	★ ★ ★
Updating:	Unclear	Content:	★ ★ ★ ★ ★
Navigation:	★ ★ ★ ★	Speed:	★ ★ ★ ★

UK

Bursting with ideas and information, this site aims to lift the profile of children's books with reviews, interviews and a variety of resources for those wanting to find out more about children's literature. The site is run from the UK but has correspondents in the United States, Canada, Australia and Europe. The colourful homepage is exceptionally busy, crammed with banners which draw your attention to prize winners, interviews, news articles and new publications. It's best approached by browsing it as if it were a magazine rather than trying to take it all in at once. The rest of the site is easily navigable from the horizontal bar which appears at the top of every screen. Fiction, non-fiction, teenage, educational, poetry and picture book all have pages of picks to themselves with reviews which include an age range where appropriate. Past picks can also be browsed. Details of books in the media such as film tie-ins can be found on the Media page. Navigation is reasonably simple although some of the labels may seem a little obscure, for instance Pic refers to picture books. Some of the resource content of the site is aimed at adults with an interest in children's literature but older children will enjoy exploring the news articles, interviews and book review sections of this vibrant site. The Buy Me link, which accompanies every book review, takes you directly to amazon.co.uk.

SPECIAL FEATURES

News includes stories featured on the homepage along with articles stretching back over the previous few months. Links to online press articles about children's literature are included. The news archives can be searched from the left of the screen, stretching back to Achuka's launch in 1997. Articles are written in a lively style, covering anything concerning children's literature, from the announcement of the Carnegie Medal winner, to the birthday celebration of a publishing house devoted to children's books

Gifts is made up of a thoughtful selection of gift suggestions.

Guides is a useful list of books and print magazines which carry children's book reviews, recommendations, guidance on choosing books and other information on children's literature.

Profiles tracks reviews and other mentions of children's authors in the press and other publications, presenting the results by author together with a booklist and any other details known about them. This is a particularly useful resource for researchers or other professionals involved in children's literature. There are plans to expand the author database to include 1,250 authors. This part of the site is protected and you will need a user name and password to gain access to Profiles. Both can be obtained by registering for Achuka's free email newsletter at the site's homepage.

Interviews are made up of a Booklist, an Authorfile which has details of the authors likes and dislikes, plus the interview itself. Achuka has interviewed a wide range of children's authors including Michael Morpurgo, Melvin Burgess and Babette Cole, to name but a few.

Chap is the slightly mystifying title for a page of books recommended for children who are having difficulty in developing their reading skills

There's much to explore at this lively site devoted to news, reviews and features about children's books.

www.geocities.com/adbooks
Adbooks

Overall rating: ★ ★ ★ ★ ★			
Classification:	Reading Group	**Readability:**	★ ★ ★
Updating:	Monthly	**Content:**	★ ★ ★ ★
Navigation:	★ ★ ★ ★	**Speed:**	★ ★ ★ ★ ★

US

Part of Yahoo's discussion group ring, Adbooks welcomes readers of young adult books who want to swap recommendations or join in email exchanges; however, there is much to explore here for those who prefer not to take an active part. This bright, fresh looking site is easy to use although the pale green font is a little hard on the eyes. First time visitors should click on the FAQ button for clear, step-by-step instructions on how the discussion group works and what's available at the site. Members include both children and adults, usually teachers or librarians, and discussion is friendly, intelligent and enthusiastic. Books are nominated for discussion by members, who then cast their votes for the final selections. The current choice, together with selections for the next few months, can be seen on the Schedule page, while selections going back to 1998 are available via Previous. Only members can take part in the discussions but registration is both free and simple. The site has a direct link to amazon.com from all books listed.

SPECIAL FEATURES

Recommendations consists of lists of recommended reading from members of the site. Some are listed under

Great Books others are listed by category, from classics to time travel. Lists vary from enthusiastic reviews to a simple title listing.

Authors leads to a set of links to homepages for authors who write for young adults, including Anne Fine, Gary Paulsen and S E Hinton.

This welcoming book discussion site offers recommendations for young adult books plus the chance to exchange views with other readers.

www.booktrusted.co.uk
Booktrusted

Overall rating: ★ ★ ★ ★			
Classification:	Info and Advice	**Readability:**	★ ★ ★ ★
Updating:	Weekly	**Content:**	★ ★ ★ ★ ★
Navigation:	★ ★ ★ ★	**Speed:**	★ ★ ★ ★

UK

Set up by the educational charity Booktrust, in association with The Young Booktrust, Booktrusted.com offers expert recommendations, advice and information on children's books, to both parents and teachers. The homepage highlights news and features together with Booktrusted's recommended reads. The links to the right of the screen under Booktrust lead to a page of information about the organisation's work, including Children's Book Week, the Bookstart initiative which focuses on books for babies, Booktrust publications and how to become a member of The Young Booktrust. The left-hand side of the screen is devoted to resources including children's bookshops, children's book organisations and a directory of publishers specialising in children's books. All the features offered by the site can be reached from the homepage. Clicking the Booktrusted.com link at the top of the page to find your next choice is the easiest way to explore the contents of this excellent site.

SPECIAL FEATURES

Advice for Parents aims at helping parents keep their children interested in reading by offering advice on how to start off, making reading fun, and how to choose books, supported by lists of recommendations for all age groups.

Children's Book Organisations links to contact details for a number of bodies which offer help, either with reading difficulties, such as the British Dyslexia Organisation, or in particular subject areas, such as the Poetry Society.

Subject Book Lists offers a sensible set of recommendations for a wide variety of reading stages, from books for babies to fiction for 14-year-olds and over. Some lists cover difficult areas such as bullying.

Recommended Titles are singled out by staff on a weekly basis for special attention. Each book is reviewed in full, with themes helpfully highlighted in the Key Words section at the top of the review, together with the age group it is likely to interest and a reading age.

Other Features include bestseller lists, details about prize, winners past and present and a diary of children's book events in the UK.

This well-researched site is an excellent source of recommendations and information on children's books for both parents and professionals concerned with promoting children's literacy.

www.cool-reads.co.uk
Cool-reads

Overall rating: ★ ★ ★ ★ ★			
Classification:	Reviews	Readability:	★ ★ ★ ★ ★
Updating:	Monthly	Content:	★ ★ ★ ★
Navigation:	★ ★ ★ ★ ★	Speed:	★ ★ ★ ★ ★

UK

Created in January 2001 by Tim Cross, then 11 years old, and his 13-year-old brother, Chris, this decidedly cool site puts many grown-up website designers to shame. Tim and Chris have put together a set of reviews for 10 to 15-year-olds, written both by themselves and by regular visitors to the site, to form a set of cool reads. Latest reviews are listed to the left of the screen while the right hand bar offers the opportunity to explore the site's reviews by theme. The main body of the homepage highlights regularly updated Top Picks plus any new websites that have taken Tim and Chris's fancy. There's a small games section at the bottom and the site also hosts a lively discussion forum. This fresh, attractive website has a very personal feel and the brothers are eager for visitors to get involved. You can see a picture of them admiring their work on the About page and there's also a set of links for Tim and Chris's favourite sites.

SPECIAL FEATURES

Reviews can be reached by clicking a theme, ranging from Action to Friends/Families, to the right of the screen. Reviews follow a set question and answer format, designed to lead the reader through the book until the verdict, in the form of a star rating, is reached. One star means 'read this book if you've got nothing better to do' while five-star books receive the ultimate accolade, a 'cool read'. Visitors to the site are encouraged to add their own comments and there's a clearly laid out submission screen for those who want to add a review, although you will have to register if you want to do either of these. Guest reviewers must say how old they are, which acts as a handy guide for other readers. The site currently, has a core of around ten reviewers including Tim and Chris.

Word Search   reached from the bottom of the homepage. The aim of this game is to find the book-related words to the right of the letter grid by running the cursor over your chosen letters in the fastest possible time. If you click on the Solve Game button you're told, quite rightly, that you've cheated.

Definitely a cool site, full of book reviews written for 10 to 15-year-olds by 10 to 15-year-olds.

www.readingmatters.co.uk
Reading Matters

Overall rating: ★ ★ ★ ★ ★			
Classification: Recommendations		**Readability:**	★ ★ ★ ★
Updating:	Unclear	**Content:**	★ ★ ★ ★ ★
Navigation:	★ ★ ★ ★	**Speed:**	★ ★ ★ ★

UK

Set up by two parents keen to share books they've enjoyed with their own children, this site houses a small but growing bank of recommendations. Most of the site's content is aimed at children and is written in an unpatronising, enthusiastic style, although occasionally the tone can be a touch prescriptive. That said, a great deal of thought has gone into the recommendations, in particular, pointers on what to read next linked to reviews, and the inclusion of quotations to give a flavour of the book. Simple and quick to find your way around, the site also has a direct link to amazon.co.uk

SPECIAL FEATURES

Ideas is a set of short articles on a variety of themes followed by a list of suggested reading. The Lists page picks up this idea with a set of booklists focussing on a particular theme.

Bookchooser   asks readers a set of questions about what they want to read, then suggests a selection of books which fit the bill.

This simple site offers a small but growing selection of thoughtful children's book recommendations.

www.wordpool.co.uk
The Word Pool

Overall rating: ★ ★ ★ ★			
Classification:	Info and Advice	**Readability:**	★ ★ ★ ★ ★
Updating:	Regularly	**Content:**	★ ★ ★ ★
Navigation:	★ ★ ★ ★ ★	**Speed:**	★ ★ ★ ★ ★

UK

Steve and Diana Kimpton have put together this informative site, aimed at parents, teachers and children's authors. Diana is an author with 11 books under her belt and has an obvious passion for spreading the word about children's books. Apart from the jolly frog, there are no graphics which speeds the site up nicely. The tone of the site is businesslike and its aim is to keep children reading and offer suggestions on where to find information to help overcome particular difficulties, whether it be special needs like dyspraxia or the everyday difficulties of learning maths. The site's simple presentation makes it easy to navigate with just one bar on the left-hand side of the screen, but a click on the Full Contents List button will display everything that is on offer. Descriptions of books are both thorough and considered and there is a section devoted to writing for children. Books can be bought via a direct link to amazon.co.uk. There's a free monthly newsletter to keep you up to date on additions to this invaluable site.

SPECIAL FEATURES

Parents Corner lists a small selection of books to help parents whose children may be suffering from particular problems, backed up with a set of links to websites which deal with a variety of issues, from special health needs such as asthma, to difficult situations such as bereavement.

Reluctant Readers offers intelligent and inventive suggestions to encourage and interest children in developing the habit of reading. It includes Terry Pratchett's Discworld novels, a selection of sports stories, graphic novels and some Riveting Reads.

Numeracy tackles a bugbear that afflicts many parents, as well as their children, with a series of short extracts from Diana Kimpton's book *A Parent's Guide to Helping with Maths*, followed by a comprehensive set of booklists for children, parents and teachers. Diana has even included instructions for games to help develop maths skills plus reviews of software and a set of links to useful sites such as Mathsphere, which aims to inject some fun into learning maths.

Big Books caters for teachers who run Literacy Hour sessions with a set of recommendations for the large format books needed to teach reading to a class of 30.

This carefully thought-out site is a boon for both parents and teachers looking for intelligent recommendations and information on children's books.

www.acs.ucalgary.ca/~dkbrown/index.html			
The Children's Literature Web Guide			
Overall rating: ★ ★ ★			
Classification: Directory		**Readability:**	★★★★
Updating: Unclear		**Content:**	★★★★
Navigation: ★★★★		**Speed:**	★★★★
CA			

Although The Children's Literature Web Guide, set up by a Canadian librarian, hasn't been updated for a while it's still well worth a visit. It's simple homepage offers a route into the plethora of sites devoted to young adult and children's books directing you to sites listed under a variety of headings, from Authors on the Web to Resources for Storytellers. There are no frills, graphics or blinking banners to distract at this site, just a carefully chosen set of links with concise descriptions of where they lead.

SPECIAL FEATURES

Stories on the Web provides a categorised index of links to children's literature published online, ranging from Classics for Young People to Songs and Poetry.

Although it hasn't been updated for a while, this site is still a useful resource for finding your way around websites devoted to children's literature.

ALSO OF INTEREST

The Book Hive
www.bookhive.org
This colourful, friendly site has Zinger the bee buzzing around recommending books for children of all ages, from babies up to 12 years old. Set up by the Public Library of Charlotte-Mecklenburg County in North Carolina, it's packed with carefully selected recommendations reviewed by librarians in a way that is both appealing and accessible to children, often backed up with children's comments on the book. Reviews are often followed by recommendations for similar books. Categories range from Realistic Fiction to Scary, and the advanced search form offers the chance to narrow your search down by age range, category and number of pages or any combination of the three. All editions of books reviewed are American.

children's publishers

Several publishers have devoted themselves to publishing children's books while others have imprints dedicated to children's literature. Many readers may have affectionate memories of Puffin books, published by Penguin, from their own childhood. In this section you'll find several publishers' sites which act as a shop window for their children's books. Although undoubtedly commercial, there's lots of advice and information for both parents and teachers on offer here, together with some fun and games for children.

www.barefootbooks.com
Barefoot Books

Overall rating: ★ ★ ★ ★ ★			
Classification:	Publishers	Readability:	★ ★ ★
Updating:	Weekly	Content:	★ ★ ★ ★ ★
Navigation:	★ ★ ★ ★	Speed:	★ ★ ★

UK 🔒

In keeping with Barefoot Books' reputation for gorgeously illustrated picture books celebrating the many cultures of the world, this site is a visual treat. It opens with a charming movie which acts as a site tour and can be overridden by clicking on either the US or the UK Site button. The site is divided into four areas. Hearth and Home is aimed at family and friends, Teachers' Tent offers a carefully graded monthly teaching idea, Artists' Café showcases the work of Barefoot's illustrators and the Storyteller's Caravan, is devoted to audio books with an audio streamed Story of the Week. All can be reached by clicking on the respective icon or via the drop down menus from the navigation bar at the top of the screen. Once the chosen area is entered, all that's on offer can be reached from the left-hand menu bar. Each screen is beautifully illustrated although the text can be a little cramped. It's worth visiting Share Our Story to gain an idea of the Barefoot philosophy which puts a good deal of emphasis on cultural diversity. Barefoot's books can be bought securely through the site.

SPECIAL FEATURES

Journeys and Pathways can be reached from either Family Hearth or Teachers' Tent. Each of the four themes in this section, Family and Friends, Seekers of Spirit, Songs of Earth and Travel, Time and Traditions, is illustrated by a book with the option to click on one of several other related themes to the right of the screen, to find more in a similar vein. The emphasis here is on helping children to explore nature, spirituality and the different cultures of the world through Barefoot's books.

Children's Party of the Month is featured in the Family Hearth section. A printable PDF file, which can be downloaded if you have Acrobat Reader software, gives details of party games, food, goodie bags and fancy dress based on a particular theme. Acrobat Reader can be downloaded, free of charge, via a link on the Party web page.

Artists' Café offers the opportunity to buy some of Barefoot's illustrators accomplished work from the Barefoot Art Shop or the Exhibition pages. This section is also the home of the Arts and Crafts Idea of the Month, held in a printable PDF file, which can be downloaded if you have Adobe Acrobat software.

Barefoot Books' charming website offers carefully chosen and beautifully illustrated books on particular themes in keeping with the publisher's philosophy of the delights of cultural diversity.

www.kidsatrandomhouse.co.uk
Kids at Random House

Overall rating: ★ ★ ★ ★			
Classification:	Publisher	Readability:	★ ★ ★ ★
Updating:	Monthly	Content:	★ ★ ★ ★
Navigation:	★ ★ ★ ★ ★	Speed:	★ ★ ★ ★

UK

A great deal of care has been taken with this bright and breezy site aimed at children, parents and teachers. The colourful icons for favourite authors and characters, from Jacqueline Wilson to Elmer, each lead to a feature carefully tailored for the relevant age group. There's a homepage for each of 5 age ranges featuring 8 books to be published in the current month plus a feature. Links for children come with sensible advice about using the internet and there's a monthly newsletter linked to a draw for signed books.

SPECIAL FEATURES

Fun Stuff has lots of quick and easy downloads for activity sheets, wallpaper and screen savers plus a selection of author interviews, book extracts, games and competitions.

Grown ups includes a set of resources and guides for parents and teachers. Teachers may find the Quentin Blake and Katie Morag notes particularly useful, although the latter is slow to download. There's a set of recommended books for Key Stage 3 plus one for very young children.

Much care has been taken in the design and content of this colourful site.

www.puffin.co.uk
Puffin

Overall rating: ★ ★ ★ ★			
Classification:	Publisher	**Readability:**	★ ★ ★ ★
Updating:	Regularly	**Content:**	★ ★ ★ ★
Navigation:	★ ★ ★ ★	**Speed:**	★ ★ ★

UK

There are lots of animations and brightly coloured graphics at Puffin's attractive website. Use the left-hand navigation bar to explore Fun Stuff, Cool Links and the Your Shout notice board, to which readers are encouraged to contribute poems, jokes and reviews of Puffin books. Some of the games on offer at Fun Stuff are rather slow to download, but the instructions for screen savers and wallpaper in Free Stuff are straightforward and easy to follow for older children. The horizontal navigation bar at the top of the screen provides the key to features about books and authors. These include a roundup of new Puffin books, a book of the month and an Author Zone. Cards give details of authors' likes, dislikes and how they set about writing. Content for children seems a little thin with the better parts of the site providing advice and information about reading to parents and teachers. Books can be bought securely at the site.

SPECIAL FEATURES

Education Zone Click on Resources in the Education Zone to find a set of teaching resources which can be photocopied for use in the classroom, including a set of notes for teaching English as a foreign language using Puffin picture books. Downloading the resource activity sheets can take

some time. The Puffin Book Club website can be reached from this part of the site and there's also the opportunity for teachers to find out about buying books at a discount in the Puffin Book Club Teacher section.

Parent's Zone Puffin have put together an excellent guide to choosing books for children. It includes practical advice on how to help your child to learn to read, how to approach difficult issues such as bereavement through books, together with outlines of the kind of books children are expected to read for Key Stages in school. The Activities option offers a selection of puzzles and crosswords.

Your Questions can be reached from both the Education and the Parents Zone. It offers advice on a range of topics including how to arrange author visits to schools and libraries, who to ask for free posters for schools and joining the Puffin Book Club.

This jolly-looking website offers thoughtful advice and information on children's books to teachers and parent as well as some fun and games for children.

www.oup.co.uk/oxed/children

Oxford University Press: Children's and Reference

Overall rating: ★ ★ ★			
Classification: Publisher		**Readability:**	★ ★ ★ ★
Updating: Regularly		**Content:**	★ ★ ★
Navigation: ★ ★ ★		**Speed:**	★ ★ ★ ★

UK

The Children's and Reference homepage of Oxford University Press's website offers a means of navigating what's available for children and teachers at the site, although you may find yourself resorting to your browser back button. The site is split into four main sections, Poetry, Dictionaries, Fiction, and Picture Books, each of which has a homepage. Content can be patchy but both Fiction and Picture Books are well worth visiting. Teachers will find the Educational/Children's Publishing dropdown menu useful for finding areas of the site that fit their interest such as the Oxford Literacy Web or the Oxford Maths Zone. Children may want to visit Children's Mini Sites for a few author interviews and sample chapters tied in to particular publications.

SPECIAL FEATURES

Fiction has an excellent Like This? Love This feature which includes suggestions for fans of J K Rowling, Phillip Pullman, Jaqueline Wilson, David Almond and Robert Swindells.

This site helps visitors find the many educational and children's areas of Oxford University Press's website although navigation can be tricky.

www.scholastic.co.uk

Scholastic

Overall rating: ★ ★ ★			
Classification: Publisher		**Readability:**	★ ★ ★ ★
Updating: Regularly		**Content:**	★ ★ ★ ★
Navigation: ★ ★ ★		**Speed:**	★ ★ ★

UK

Primarily an educational publisher, Scholastic has aimed most of the content of this site squarely at teachers. New publications of teachers' magazines and resources are highlighted on the homepage, with links to detailed descriptions. The rest of the site can be navigated from the Choose a Destination box or from the colourful bars at either side of the screen. The Children's Zone has a link to the *Goosebumps* and *Babysitters Club* sites plus pages devoted to the *Horrible* series but sometimes promises more than it delivers with Cool Sites offering very little other than links to Scholastic-related sites. Speed can be a problem.

SPECIAL FEATURES

Teachers Resources offers a facility to search Scholastic's catalogue. Books, magazines and resources packs can be bought securely online and discounts are available.

Book Fairs links to a Scholastic website aimed at encouraging and helping teachers to run book fairs in their schools.

This site will primarily be of interest to teachers looking for reliable resources packs.

www.usborne.com
Usborne Publishing

Overall rating: ★ ★ ★			
Classification:	Publisher	Readability:	★ ★ ★ ★
Updating:	Regularly	Content:	★ ★ ★
Navigation:	★ ★ ★	Speed:	★ ★ ★

UK

Usborne Publishing's attractively illustrated entertaining yet educational books are popular with both children and parents. The homepage of their website offers news of the current month's new books with lots of opportunities to sample before you buy plus national curriculum information where appropriate. The text of some extracts is a little difficult to read but this feature does offer a chance to view layout and illustrations. The rest of the site can be explored from the left-hand navigation bar which lists subject areas from Music to Sport, each of which has its own homepage. Books can be bought via a direct link to amazon.co.uk. Those interested in setting up a home-based business selling Usborne books should click the Usborne Books at Home link.

SPECIAL FEATURES

Quicklinks is the route into Usborne's internet-linked books on subjects ranging from art to science. Images and information can be downloaded from the books and there are clear instructions to help you do so.

This bright, attractive site offers the chance to sample Usborne's range of award-winning educational books.

authors and characters

There's lots of fun to be had here with sites devoted to well-loved characters such as Dr Seuss, Tintin and, of course, Harry Potter, as well as a few favourite authors. Many of the sites have lots of pictures and animations which make them enormous fun but also mean that for those who don't use a broadband service they often take some time to load and response can be a little slow. If your browser has a caching facility, you may well find that loading is faster on subsequent visits.

Sites in this section appear in alphabetical order.

asterix

www.asterix.tm.fr
The Official Asterix Website

Overall rating: ★ ★ ★			
Classification:	Official Site	Readability:	★ ★ ★ ★
Updating:	Monthly	Content:	★ ★ ★
Navigation:	★ ★ ★	Speed:	★ ★ ★ ★

FR

There's much for Asterix fans to enjoy here but a good deal of patience is required as both loading and response are very slow. Most of the content can be explored from the icons to the left of the screen. Click on Characters for profiles of favourites like Sarsaparilla or Dogmatix. Contributions to The Forum, reached from the right of the screen, are lively, passionate and truly international. If you want to join in, click on Send a Message, rather than New Message as the text suggests. You can explore Asterix further, with nine pages of links to websites throughout the world. To return to the homepage at any time, click the Asterix logo at the top left-hand corner.

SPECIAL FEATURES

The Asterix Files is undoubtedly the site's best feature. Every month a new Asterix story is posted on the homepage and added to the Files, all of which are accessible from the top of the Characters pages.

The World of Asterix is a glossary in the Characters pages which explains Asterix's historical context.

Great fun for Asterix fans but patience is required.

roald dahl

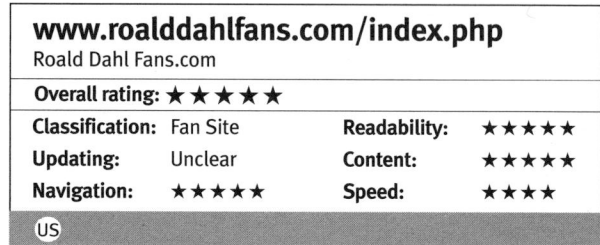

www.roalddahlfans.com/index.php			
Roald Dahl Fans.com			
Overall rating: ★ ★ ★ ★ ★			
Classification: Fan Site		Readability:	★ ★ ★ ★ ★
Updating: Unclear		Content:	★ ★ ★ ★ ★
Navigation: ★ ★ ★ ★ ★		Speed:	★ ★ ★ ★
US			

Set up by Kristine Howard, an ardent Roald Dahl fan, this site may not include the fancy graphics of many Dahl sites but it can't be beaten for its attention to the tiniest details, even to the extent of including Roald Dahl's *Guide to Railway Safety* under Dahl's Works. The site includes a lengthy biography of Dahl, together with links to interviews and a set of detailed Timelines covering his work and personal life. Kristine has included the author's adult short stories, together with the films with which he was connected in the Dahl's Work section. There are a couple of crossword puzzles and plenty of trivia quizzes in Fun Stuff, although there's no chance of cheating as answers to the questions are not supplied. There's also an illustrated account of Kristine's visit to the Roald Dahl Children's Museum in Buckinghamshire. The FAQ section for the site has a slightly waspish tone in places but is nevertheless, a great source of information on specific questions. The site is extremely easy to navigate and there is a good deal of cross-referencing by hyperlink throughout. Younger fans might prefer to visit the Roald Dahl Official site at www.roalddahl.com/index2.htm which has some lovely graphics but can be very slow and lacks this site's loving attention to detail.

SPECIAL FEATURES

Dahl's Work contains extraordinarily detailed information on Dahl's books, short stories and the films to which he contributed. Individual entries include cross-referencing to reviews, teaching resources and other information within the site, plus a description, publication details and details of any prizes won. The Anthologies page lists all anthologies which include a Dahl story.

In The Classroom features a well thought out page of information on how to set about homework based on Dahl's work, as well as a wide-ranging set of teaching resources. Many of the lesson plans and classroom activities have been contributed to the site by teachers from around the world. The Teachers section also includes a links to a few online teaching resource websites.

A true labour of love, this site is crammed with information on Roald Dahl including some excellent teaching resource materials.

terry deary

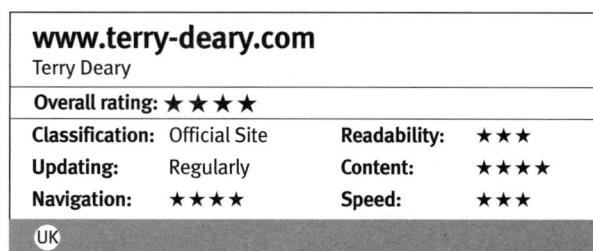

www.terry-deary.com
Terry Deary

Overall rating: ★ ★ ★ ★			
Classification:	Official Site	**Readability:**	★ ★ ★
Updating:	Regularly	**Content:**	★ ★ ★ ★
Navigation:	★ ★ ★ ★	**Speed:**	★ ★ ★

UK

Lots of fun for fans of Terry Deary's Horrible Histories, True Mysteries and Shivers, to name just a few of his creations. Details of all Terry's books can be found in the House of Books, together with some extracts. The House of Adventure is the place to visit for news of TV series, roadshows and plays. The House of Fun jokes page features Terry's particular brand of punning humour but, sadly, although The House of Chat offers lots of encouragement to post messages at the Young ABC Tales website, complete with a link, it no longer exists. The House of Mystery offers a web story and an interactive mystery, both of which can be downloaded if you have Acrobat Reader software, easily installed free of charge via the site. The whole site is presented in Terry Deary's inimitable style, its only drawback being the lengthy downloading of some story files. The Club House is currently closed to new members, but it's still possible to explore features such as the Party Page, for Deary-inspired games, food and stories, and read hints on writing your own Horrible Histories. You can also send Terry a question although any on school projects are very firmly banned.

Lots of fun for Horrible History fans.

doctor seuss

www.seussville.com/seussville		
Seussville		
Overall rating: ★ ★ ★ ★ ★		
Classification: Official Site	**Readability:**	★ ★ ★ ★ ★
Updating: Regularly	**Content:**	★ ★ ★ ★ ★
Navigation: ★ ★ ★ ★	**Speed:**	★ ★ ★
US		

There's loads of fun to be had here with lots of games and printable activity sheets. The colourful graphics will keep young children entertained while games load. Click on Playground to find a wide variety of games. These range from interactive, for which you will need Shockwave software, easily downloaded free of charge via the link at the Seussville site, to Print and Play activities, for which you'll need Acrobat Reader. As with all sites with a high graphic content Seussville requires a reasonable degree of patience but you do have a choice between high and low bandwidth. Navigation can be a little tricky at times but that said this site is a treat for all ages. Seussville is a sub-site of Random House publishers and there is a link back to the American version of Kids @ Random at the bottom of the homepage.

Just the thing for a rainy day, this site is packed with entertainment for fans of Doctor Seuss.

harry potter

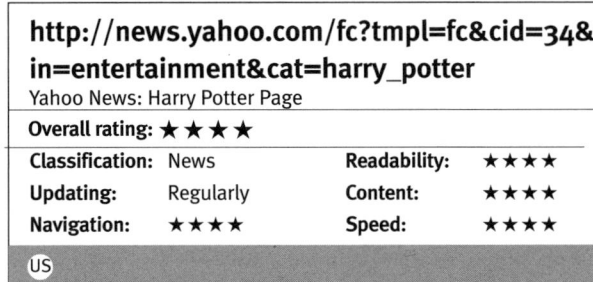

http://news.yahoo.com/fc?tmpl=fc&cid=34& in=entertainment&cat=harry_potter		
Yahoo News: Harry Potter Page		
Overall rating: ★ ★ ★ ★		
Classification: News	**Readability:**	★ ★ ★ ★
Updating: Regularly	**Content:**	★ ★ ★ ★
Navigation: ★ ★ ★ ★	**Speed:**	★ ★ ★ ★
US		

Not the best-looking site for Potter fans but as a route into the burgeoning number of fan sites, plus up to the minute news items, this site is hard to beat. There are links to the latest news stories accompanied by notice boards to air your views. Other links lead to recently published features, opinion pieces and the many pages devoted to Harry Potter and J K Rowling at Yahoo!. Related Web Site Links offers a small selection of Potter websites, including further directories.

SPECIAL FEATURES

Yahoo! Categories: Harry Potter Beginning with a list of the most popular websites, this is a well-maintained directory of links to both official and fan sites. The site also has a Yahoo! Categories: J K Rowling link.

Yahooligans: Harry Potter Series Part of Yahoo's Web Guide for Kids, this is a directory of links to Potter sites for kids.

A well-maintained site for those desperate for breaking news on Harry Potter.

redwall abbey

www.Redwall.org/dave/news.php			
Redwall Abbey			
Overall rating: ★ ★ ★			
Classification: Official Site		**Readability:**	★ ★ ★ ★
Updating: Regularly		**Content:**	★ ★ ★
Navigation: ★ ★ ★ ★		**Speed:**	★ ★ ★ ★
UK			

This site has lots of friendly content and attractive illustrations. The homepage has news of developments at Redwall Abbey with pieces by Brian in Biography, BJ's Ideas and A Good Yarn. The Library section contains book synopses plus comments from fans, while the Gallery has charming illustrations. There are also several crossword puzzles. Information about Redwall-related gifts can be found in the Giftshop. The site is easily navigated from the left-hand bar or via the Redwall Transporter box at the bottom of each page.

SPECIAL FEATURES

Ask Brian Q&As put to Brian by visitors to the site.

Snowfur's Redwall Encyclopedia offers a link to a separate website containing an extensive reference guide to the Redwall series plus lots of Redwall links. Well worth a visit.

Readers Club Registration details for the official fan club.

The official Redwall site offers friendly articles by Brian Jacques plus useful links to other Redwall sites.

tintin

www.tintin.com/uk			
Tintin.com			
Overall rating: ★ ★ ★ ★			
Classification: Official Site		**Readability:**	★ ★ ★
Updating: Unclear		**Content:**	★ ★ ★ ★ ★
Navigation: ★ ★ ★ ★		**Speed:**	★ ★ ★ ★
BE			

The Hergé Foundation are notoriously protective of Tintin and this, together with the excellent quality of reproduction, makes the official site the best stop for fans of the intrepid boy reporter. To view it, you will need Flash plug-in software which can be downloaded via the site, free of charge. There is much to delight older Tintin fans at this site, at whom much of its content is aimed. Click first on The Adventures of Tintin then on the Adventures of Hergé for a biography of Tintin's creator while What About Us in Comic Books offers a chance to see Hergé's less well-known creations, Quicke and Flupke. Details of any new developments can be found at the Information Kiosk. The English translation in some parts of the site is a little eccentric.

SPECIAL FEATURES

The Dossiers give detailed background information on a selection of Tintin stories including changes in artistic technique and historical background.

This official site is the best place to find out about Tintin on the internet although much of its content is aimed at older fans.

OTHER SITES OF INTEREST

Melvin Burgess Homepage
http://web.onetel.net.uk/~melvinburgess/index.htm

The homepage of this controversial author of young adult novels is well worth visiting for chatty and informative news which often includes a robust and well-argued defence against the latest criticisms aimed at him. It also houses an interesting set of questions and answers put together by Burgess from several interviews and a set of short essays on each of his books describing how he came to write them and the thinking behind their structure, themes and characterisation. The site has a few articles written by Burgess about writing and the development of teenage fiction which are more likely to appeal to teachers and parents that young adult readers.

The Peter Rabbit Official Website
www.peterrabbit.co.uk

This site includes information about Beatrix Potter, where to buy gifts, news and a competition, but click on Fun! for the best bit. Once this part of the site has loaded you can either click on the site map or, much more fun, pass your mouse over the characters to decide who to visit. Tom Kitten's Playground has word games and puzzles based on Beatrix Potter's books or you might like to send one of Jemima Puddleduck's charming cards. There are excerpts from Squirrel Nutkin's videos to be watched although you'll need Apple Quicktime for this, downloadable free of charge via the site. Gifts, books, videos and CD Roms can all be bought securely. This is a site for young children who will love the delightful animations and soundtrack.

Philip Pullman: His Dark Materials
www.randomhouse.com/features/pullman/philippullman/index.html

This site should please fans of Philip Pullman's gripping fantasy trilogy, *His Dark Materials*. Along with a biography of the author the site has an interview with him about writing the trilogy and a page devoted to the workings of the alethiometer, the mysterious divining tool which appears in the books. There are pages for each part of the trilogy which contain readers' and teachers' guides, together with a glossary and a cast of characters. An excerpt is available to be read on screen or, if you have Real Player software, you can listen to it. The audio clip takes around five minutes to download but is well worth the wait.

Winnie the Pooh
www.just-pooh.com

Fans of Winnie the Pooh can visit the 100 Acre Wood and click on their favourite character to read all about them at this charmingly illustrated site which also contains a short history of Poohsticks bridge. The site features an extract from the Tao of Pooh plus story extracts. There's a quiz in the Fun section and ecards can be sent with a message of your choice. Traditionalists may be disappointed by the short Walt Disney audio clips on offer in the 100 Acre Wood.

reading group resources

reading groups

For many readers, being a member of a reading group has become an essential part of both their social and their reading lives. Oprah Winfrey's announcement that she was winding up her book club was met with much hand-wringing by American publishers who knew that they would have a guaranteed bestseller on their hands if she picked one of their books. The internet is an excellent source of information for reading groups wanting guidance or information but as yet, with the notable exception of *Guardian Unlimited*'s books discussion group, online groups haven't taken off in the UK in the same way as they have in the US.

Listed below you'll find sites specifically designed to provide resources for reading groups plus a couple of reading group sites and a directory of American groups in case you fancy a little transatlantic exchange of views.

http://books.guardian.co.uk/readinggroup/0,6704,137656,00.html
Guardian Unlimited: Reading Group

Overall rating: ★ ★ ★ ★ ★			
Classification:	Reading Group	Readability:	★ ★ ★ ★
Updating:	Monthly	Content:	★ ★ ★ ★ ★
Navigation:	★ ★ ★ ★ ★	Speed:	★ ★ ★ ★

US R

The homepage of *Guardian Unlimited*'s reading group spells out the way it works before listing the current book under discussion, followed by details of next month's choice and an invitation to suggest future titles. Past exchanges can be explored, further down the page, to get some idea of the way discussions go before joining in. Book choices range from Paul Auster's *Timbuktu* to Dostoyevsky's *Crime and Punishment*. Each choice is supported by links to relevant material including reviews, a link to the online text, where appropriate, and a link to amazon.co.uk. There's a strong and intelligent engagement with both the book and with other contributors on the discussion boards, and a hard core of regular visitors lends a nice feeling of community. You will need to register with *Guardian Unlimited* to post your own comments but this is both quick and free.

The discussions boards at this lively web page have a real feeling of engagement and community.

www.bbc.co.uk/arts/books/club
BBC Book Club Online

Overall rating: ★ ★ ★ ★			
Classification:	Reading Group	Readability:	★ ★ ★ ★ ★
Updating:	Monthly	Content:	★ ★ ★ ★
Navigation:	★ ★ ★	Speed:	★ ★ ★

UK

The current month's book choice together with programme broadcast times are displayed on the homepage of this section of the BBC's website which acts as a companion to Radio 4's *Book Club*. Free registration is required for the message board which is intended as a forum for discussion. Forthcoming book choices and dates are listed on the page and there is a link at the bottom which gives you the opportunity to suggest a question to be put to guest authors at forthcoming *Book Club* discussions or to put your name down to attend.

SPECIAL FEATURES

Join a Book Club offers friendly, well researched advice on setting up a book club.

Past Book Clubs offers a choice of past *Book Club* selections, each of which has a synopsis, a transcript of the programme, an extract and a set of well-chosen links to reviews, interviews, author websites and other information useful for discussion.

A well researched companion to Radio 4's popular Book Club programme.

www.penguin.co.uk/static/packages/uk/readers/index.html

Penguin Readers Group

Overall rating: ★ ★ ★ ★			
Classification:	Reading Group	**Readability:**	★ ★ ★ ★
Updating:	Monthly	**Content:**	★ ★ ★ ★ ★
Navigation:	★ ★ ★ ★	**Speed:**	★ ★ ★

UK R

The Readers' Group section of Penguin's website aims to provide a resource for reading groups offering advice, news, and information about books published by the company, rather than an online reading group. You will need to register both to enter this part of the Penguin site and to qualify for the discounts and freebies on offer but registration is both simple and free. The homepage focuses on an author of the month one of whose books is suggested for groups to read and discuss, with other suggestions highlighted in the Themed feature. The Author of the Month feature usually includes an interview, extracts from the book and a profile of the author's other work. The Notice Board is the place to visit for monthly articles, reviews and information posted by readers' groups. There's lots of encouragement for participation with a Readers Group Directory, free books to review and the opportunity to suggest ideas. A free newsletter keeps you in touch with new features at the site. The site is easily navigable from the bar to the left of the screen, although the font on the buttons is not for the myopic. Past monthly features are archived and easily accessible through Bookshelf. Response can be a little slow.

SPECIAL FEATURES

Themed suggests concepts as a basis for group discussions, such as memory and memories. There are links to suggested books to fit the chosen theme, including an introduction to the book, extracts, reviews, biographical details and reader's comments.

Cult Choice is author Toby Litt's monthly recommendation of a book which is a little outside the mainstream. Past choices include Sylvia Plath's *Ariel* and Dashiell Hammett's *The Maltese Falcon*.

Group of the Month is a monthly feature in which a reading group offers an account of its discussions. One particular book is chosen as a focus for the article which includes a synopsis and record of the group's discussion.

Notice Board can include articles by authors on their own reading and readers' group experiences together with informative articles about resources for reading groups and competition results.

An attractive site offering a forum for groups through its friendly notice board, with lots of suggestions for books to read and discuss.

www.randomhouse.co.uk/readersgroup/special.htm

Random House Readers Group

Overall rating: ★ ★ ★ ★			
Classification:	Reading Group	Readability:	★ ★ ★ ★
Updating:	Monthly	Content:	★ ★ ★ ★
Navigation:	★ ★ ★ ★ ★	Speed:	★ ★ ★ ★

UK

Random House was the first publisher to produce a set of printed reading group guides in the UK and they have recently set up a section in their main website dedicated to reading groups. The fresh, bright pages include a monthly wide-ranging Special Feature, Hot Tips for running groups sent in by members, favourite recipes in Host with the Most and a competition. A free monthly newsletter requires registration but you won't need to register to use the site.

SPECIAL FEATURES

Hot Spot Each month readers can quiz an author about their work. Future 'hotspot' authors are posted well in advance.

Reading Guides include a synopsis, often identifying the book's major themes, followed by a set of discussion questions which refer closely to the book. The quality can vary a little with some guides including up to twenty detailed questions while others stop at six. Authors include Louis de Bernières, Anne Tyler, Angela Carter and Ian McEwan.

A new fresh-looking site set up by Random House as a resource for reading groups.

www.you-reading-group.co.uk/

You Reading Group

Overall rating: ★ ★ ★ ★			
Classification:	Reading Group	Readability:	★ ★ ★ ★
Updating:	Monthly	Content:	★ ★ ★ ★
Navigation:	★ ★ ★ ★	Speed:	★ ★ ★

UK

This website is an extension of the immensely successful reading group feature in the *Mail on Sunday's* YOU magazine. Both the current book of the month and the previous month's choice are featured on the homepage, alongside buttons leading to a set of materials designed to get a discussion off the ground. Most of the materials, which include a review, an interview, a brief author biography and discussion questions, are stimulating and well-written although the If You Like This…. feature can be disappointingly restricted to the author's previous books or just a few other titles. The site is easy to find your way around with a menu at the top of the page offering the chance to browse past choices, read advice on setting up your own group and submit a review. Book choices usually fall into literary fiction with a couple of forays into biography. All choices, past and present, can be bought through the site at highly competitive prices.

This online extension to the Mail on Sunday's *YOU reading group feature offers discussion materials for both past and present book choices.*

OTHER SITES OF INTEREST

Oprah's book Club
www.oprah.com/obc/obc_landing.jhtml

Oprah's Book Club became an immensely popular part of her show before she called a halt in 2002 but there are plans to reintroduce it and it may well be up and running by the time you read this. Meanwhile, there's much to explore in the Book Club Library which has archives of past choices dating back to 1995, together with discussion materials including extracts, interviews, reviews and questions. The book selections are often quite challenging, ranging from Barbara Kingsolver's *Poisonwood Bible* to Bernard Schlink's *The Reader*. The Message Boards are still open and worth a visit for their users' passionate engagement both with each other and with the book discussed.

Yahoo Clubs: Reading Groups
http://dir.clubs.yahoo.com/Entertainment——Arts/ Humanities/Books_and_Writing/Reading_Groups/

Yahoo Clubs plays hosts to well over 1000 reading groups. The directory offers the choice to browse the entire list or to browse by genre or by culture. Lists are presented in order of popularity. Some groups choose to specialise in areas such as Russian literature, while others take a more general approach. Although the majority of groups originate in the US, many others have been set up by people from other countries and membership is truly international. Each club has its own homepage where discussions and members' details can be browsed before deciding whether to join. You'll need to register with Yahoo in order to join a reading group.

reading group guides

Aware of the huge number of avid reading group members who are keen for information on which to base their discussions, American publishers have long been producing reading group guides to accompany their books. Many of these are now available online. Although the guides are based on American editions, most of the books are available in Britain and, with a little resourcefulness, the guides can be adapted to suit UK editions, if necessary. British publishers have now joined in and several UK publishing sites also include reading group guides.

www.readinggroupguides.com			
Reading Group Guides.com			
Overall rating: ★ ★ ★ ★			
Classification: Information		**Readability:**	★ ★ ★ ★
Updating: Monthly		**Content:**	★ ★ ★ ★ ★
Navigation: ★ ★ ★ ★		**Speed:**	★ ★ ★ ★
(US)			

Nearly every American publisher has a reading group spot on their websites, but Reading Group Guides.com has collected many of the guides scattered across the internet into one convenient place. Although the main body of the site is made up of the guides there are also pages in Advice and Ideas on setting up and running groups together with ideas contributed by reading groups and even a recipe of the month. The Roundtable section focuses on the experiences of reading groups including lists of favourite books and answers to questions such as how to get quieter members more involved. A monthly newsletter keeps you up to date on new guides, and other additions to the site. The guides may include excerpts, an interview with the author, an author biography or reviews but will always offer a detailed synopsis of the book together with a set of discussion questions. Guides can be browsed by subject or searched alphabetically by author or title.

An excellent one-stop site for reading groups looking for guides and advice.

OTHER SITES OF INTEREST

US

amazon.com
www.amazon.com
Reached from the left-hand menu bar of the books homepage, Amazon.com's reading group page lists recommendations, including biography, business and history as well as fiction. Click on your chosen title to display the Amazon book review, then click the reading group guide link to the left to display the guide. Guides include a brief synopsis plus a list of discussion points which closely follow the text.

Harper Collins: Reading Guides
www.harpercollins.com/hc/readers/
Guides at HarperCollins American website range from modern classics, such as Sylvia Plath's *Ariel*, to bestsellers such as Rebecca Wells' *Divine Secrets of the Ya-Ya Sisterhood*. A smaller selection of non-fiction guides includes Susan Faludi's *Stiffed* alongside the bestselling *Perfect Storm*. Guides include a plot summary identifying the book's themes, a set of discussion questions and an author biography although the balance between these three sections varies considerably.

Penguin Putnam
www.penguinputnam.com/
Penguin includes over 100 reading group guides alongside advice on setting up, in the reading groups section of its American site. The guides cover both novels and non-fiction by a wide range of authors, including Paul Auster, Helen Fielding and Gabriel Garcia Marquez. Each guide includes a short synopsis, an author biography, a set of discussion questions and, in many cases, an interview with the author about the book. An email newsletter will inform you when new guides are added.

Simon and Schuster
www.simonsays.com/Sections/Areas.cfm?AreaID=4&RecDisplay=10&ORDER=PUB
Simon and Schuster's American website houses an extensive list of reading guides in its Reading Group Resources section, including a surprisingly large number of business books. Up to fifty guides can be listed at a time and there is an option to read an excerpt from each book. Guides may include a synopsis and an author biography or simply consist of a set of discussion points. Authors include Robert Hellenga, Frank McCourt and Rose Tremain.

Time Warner
www.twbookmark.com/books/reading_guides.html
The reading groups page of Time Warner's American publishing site offers three ways of browsing its bank of reading group guides; by author, by title or by category. The guides are simply a set of questions around which a discussion may be based but there is the opportunity to read a chapter online. Authors include Anita Shreve, Helen Dunmore and Jody Shields.

UK

Bloomsbury Magazine: Bloomsbury Reading Club
www.bloomsburymagazine.com
Click on the Readers link at the top of the main homepage of Bloomsbury's site to reach a set of guides for books ranging from Andrea Barrett's novel, *The Voyage of the Narwhal*, to Jenny Diski's travelogue, *Skating to Antarctica*. The guides follow a set pattern and include a lengthy synopsis identifying the book's major themes, a set of discussion questions, a brief author biography and suggested further reading. The site also includes advice on setting up and running a group together with a notice board. Discounts and competitions are open to members of the Bloomsbury Reading Club and membership is free.

Books at Transworld: Reading Guides
www.booksattransworld.co.uk
The Put Up Your Feet section of Transworld's website has a small selection of reading group guides on books by authors ranging from Joanne Harris to Willy Russell. The guides can be variable with some consisting of a brief author biography, a plot summary, an interview with the author, a set of discussion points and suggestions for further reading, while others are simply a lengthy synopsis. It's worth checking the author interview and extracts section of the magazine for further information on the book.

literary resources and reference

literary resources

Whether your trying to do your own homework or setting it for someone else, the internet offers a wide range of literary resources which can help you track down the information you're after. The sites reviewed below range from annotated directories of links to literature or book-related sites, including genres such as crime, science fiction and poetry, to sites offering advice on studying literature or information on all aspects of the book world, from how to find a publisher to running events on National Poetry Day. Here, as with many websites devoted to books, although some sites are undoubtedly commercial, others have been lovingly compiled by enthusiasts.

www.bookspot.com
Book Spot

Overall rating: ★ ★ ★ ★ ★			
Classification:	Directory	**Readability:**	★ ★ ★ ★
Updating:	Unclear	**Content:**	★ ★ ★ ★ ★
Navigation:	★ ★ ★	**Speed:**	★ ★ ★ ★ ★

US

Part of a network of special interest directory sites, Book Spot acts as a gateway to a multitude of book-related websites, most of them American but with a smattering of sites based in other English-speaking countries. The homepage provides a flavour of what's available, highlighting a selection of links to author and genre sites plus a few must-see sites, while the yellow menu bar lists four major categories of information. What to Read directs you to book reviews, prize winners, recommended reading lists and books published online. Genre Corner lists specialist pages including science fiction, young adult and romance. Where to Buy has links to shops including some specialists and a selection of American price comparison sites. Behind the Books offers access to publishers, authors and discussion groups. Although your eye is inevitably drawn to the bright yellow bar, there's lots more on offer at this extensive site. Both the Reference Desk and Book News drop-down menus at the top of the screen include links to a variety of pages which do not appear on the yellow bar and yet more pages can be found in the More to Explore box away from the homepage. A free monthly newsletter keeps you up to date on new links. Although some of the review sites are a little parochial, this site offers an excellent guide to interesting and noteworthy book sites.

SPECIAL FEATURES

Reference Desk Choose a link from this drop down-menu and a set of options appears guiding you to a range of reference pages which includes maps, biographies, dictionaries and genealogy as well as a set of American library site links and ask an expert databases.

Editor's Picks found at the top of the homepage, guides you to some of the more out of the way book websites.

Questions and Answers reached from the More to Explore box to the right of the page, this section of the site is well worth visiting for answers to questions such as 'Where can I hear authors reading online?' or 'Where can I find out about copyright information?'

This extensive directory takes a little time to explore but rewards you by leading you to a multitude of excellent book sites, many of them American.

http://andromeda.rutgers.edu/~jlynch/Lit
Literary Resources on the Net

Overall rating: ★ ★ ★ ★ ★			
Classification: Directory		**Readability:**	★ ★ ★ ★
Updating: Unclear		**Content:**	★ ★ ★ ★ ★
Navigation: ★ ★ ★ ★		**Speed:**	★ ★ ★ ★

US

This detailed directory of internet literary resources is an invaluable tool for literature students. The homepage lists the subject areas available and offers a search facility for all but the eighteenth-century listings, which form a separate archive. The first half of the list deals with literature chronologically, beginning with Classical & Biblical and ending with Twentieth Century British and Irish writing. The second part of the list deals with a variety of areas, including American Literature, Ethnicities & Nationalities, which includes Native American, Latino, Jewish and Black Studies, and Other National Literatures, which covers the rest of the word. Other subjects include Bibliography & the History of the Book, Women's Literature & Feminism and Theatre & Drama. Listings are thoroughly annotated with accurate, but concise descriptions of websites.

SPECIAL FEATURES

The Eighteenth-Century page also includes listings for other subjects, such as philosophy and art, and has its own search engine.

Although primarily aimed at academics, this directory site has much to interest other literature enthusiasts.

http://www.bedfordstmartins.com/litlinks
Litlinks

Overall rating: ★ ★ ★ ★ ★			
Classification: Info/Publisher		**Readability:**	★ ★ ★ ★ ★
Updating: Unclear		**Content:**	★ ★ ★ ★ ★
Navigation: ★ ★ ★ ★		**Speed:**	★ ★ ★ ★

US

Put together by the American academic publishers Bedford/St Martins, this site is largely aimed at literature students but it's likely to be of interest to anyone who enjoys reading literature critically. The main part of the site is split into five sections: fiction, drama, poetry, essays and critical theory. Click on any one of the corresponding coloured blocks to display a set of writers published by Bedford/St Martins, ranging from Annie Proulx to Plato. Each author has a page which includes a biographical essay supported by links to other sites. Above the coloured subject bar, there are links to other parts of the site, including a directory of literary sites organised by period, a list of introductory books to studying literature under Related Texts plus a link to a separate site on research techniques.

SPECIAL FEATURES

Reading... At the bottom left-hand corner of each genre's author directory, there's a link to a page of intelligent and well thought out discussion points around which to base a critical reading of a text.

Literary Periods is reached from the top right of subject screens, or under Other Links on the main homepage.

Beginning with the Medieval period and ending with Contemporary Literature: 1945 to the Present, these pages offer an annotated set of links to a range of literary sites, most of which are attached to universities.

Research Room takes you to the Bedford Researcher site, run by Mike Palmquist, a Bedford/St. Martins author, as an online companion to his book. It offers advice on researching literature, both in the library and on the internet. Advice on research is written for American students and although much of it is appropriate to students of other countries, it's probably best to check with your university if you intend to use the site as a study aid.

An excellent resource for both students and readers who want to take a more active part in their enjoyment of literature.

www.poetrysociety.org.uk			
Poetry Society			
Overall rating: ★ ★ ★ ★ ★			
Classification:	Organisation	**Readability:**	★ ★ ★ ★
Updating:	Regularly	**Content:**	★ ★ ★ ★ ★
Navigation:	★ ★ ★	**Speed:**	★ ★ ★ ★

UK

The Poetry Society website provides an excellent resource for teachers, librarians, readers and writers of poetry. You'll need to scan all three columns of the homepage to see all that's available at the site, from news and magazine-style features to information about events and competitions plus educational and library resources. A visit to the About Us page explains the Society's background and what it has to offer, including information about current projects, the National Poetry Competition and National Poetry Day. There are excerpts from the Society's publications, Poetry Review and Poetry News, plus a list of forthcoming poetry books in the UK, although no editorial content to complement it. The site has a shop where Poetry Society publications and resources can be bought securely. Those wishing to join the Society can do so online.

SPECIAL FEATURES

Links includes Lively Links which acts as a notice board listing events, work opportunities and calls for proposals. Links to other websites range from sites devoted to particular poets including Simon Armitage, Carol Ann Duffy and Siegfried Sassoon to sites aimed at helping poets develop their skills.

Education leads to a set of attractively presented resources aimed at helping those teaching poetry in schools. It includes information about poetryclass, the society's training programme led by published poets, a list of resources for teachers which can be bought securely online from the Poetry Society shop, and links to sites aimed at getting young people writing.

Library Room has information and resources aimed at librarians who wish to promote poetry. It includes practical tips on developing a 'poetry friendly library', suggestions for poetry books to be kept in stock, information about events aimed at librarians and a set of links to recommended sites.

An invaluable resource for poets, readers, teachers and librarians.

www.sfsite.com
The SF Site

Overall rating: ★★★★★			
Classification:	Directory	**Readability:**	★★★★
Updating:	Fortnightly	**Content:**	★★★★★
Navigation:	★★★★★	**Speed:**	★★★★

CA

The SF Site combines its own rich editorial content with a comprehensive directory of other science fiction and horror websites. New reviews, interviews and columns are featured on the homepage. The left-hand menu acts as a guide to other new content and also includes an impressive set of featured sites to which The SF Site plays host, including the magazine *Interzone*. The Site Index is a bit intimidating for first-time visitors but the Contents List offers more of a taster of what's available, with highlighted reviews, interviews, author booklists, columns, fan sites plus an index or the facility to search a section alphabetically where appropriate. Headings for the extensive links index appear at the bottom of this page.

SPECIAL FEATURES

Author Reading Lists features recommendations by authors ranging from Terry Pratchett to Kim Stanley Robinson.

Links cover a wide of related websites, ranging from fan sites and other ezines, to publishers and writing resources.

This site combines its own rich content with an extensive directory of links to other science fiction and horror websites.

www.booktrust.org.uk
Booktrust

Overall rating: ★ ★ ★ ★			
Classification:	Information	Readability:	★ ★ ★ ★
Updating:	Daily	Content:	★ ★ ★ ★
Navigation:	★ ★ ★ ★ ★	Speed:	★ ★ ★ ★

UK

Booktrust is a charity promoting reading in the UK. Their website offers a variety of routes into information about the book world, from advice on getting published to lists of literary prize winners. The homepage highlights some of the main features which include a website devoted to children's books, Bookmates, a small reading group section, and an events listing. A daily Book News bulletin can be found via Publishers. There are also links to information about Booktrust plus links to other book organisations.

SPECIAL FEATURES

Bookstart A project to promote and provide information on the importance of books in the development of young babies. This section of the site guides you through the aims of the project and includes tips for parents and carers together with information on how to get your own Bookstart pack.

Factsheets currently includes an article on getting published, a list of grants and awards for writers, and details of useful organisations and information on finding copyright holders.

This site offers an invaluable source of information for all aspects of the UK book world.

www.pmpoetry.com
pmpoetry

Overall rating: ★ ★ ★ ★			
Classification:	Directory	Readability:	★ ★ ★ ★
Updating:	Unclear	Content:	★ ★ ★ ★
Navigation:	★ ★ ★ ★	Speed:	★ ★ ★ ★ ★

US

Patrick Martin's lovingly assembled directory of poetry websites will interest both readers and writers alike. There are seven main sections, each containing a page of annotated links, ranging from online magazines which publish poetry to Poets and Collections, both of which list sites featuring poets such as Dante and Elizabeth Barrett Browning as well as those publicising their own work. Patrick actively encourages feedback and there's the opportunity to recommend sites for consideration. He's also included a small selection of his own poems.

SPECIAL FEATURES

Poetry Around the World includes links to Eastern European, Indian, Australian, New Zealand and South African literature sites.

Organisations lists useful sites such as poetry societies and writing programmes.

An invaluable directory of websites for both poetry lovers and aspiring poets.

www.twbooks.co.uk		
Tangled Web UK		
Overall rating: ★ ★ ★ ★		
Classification: Information	**Readability:**	★ ★ ★
Updating: Weekly	**Content:**	★ ★ ★ ★
Navigation: ★ ★ ★	**Speed:**	★ ★ ★ ★
UK		

Heralded by Ian Rankin as 'a tremendous resource', the Tangled Web offers an extensive bank of information on crime fiction for both writers and readers, ranging from Book Digests, a database of synopses for crime novels published in the UK since 1996, to Crime Scene, which covers a wide range of topics, from announcements of prize winners to author interviews. The Weblinks section in Crime Scene enticingly includes links to sites such as America's Most Wanted under Tools of the Trade, although some of these seem to be broken. A visit to the Help page is useful for navigation hints as the site's drop down lists and pop-up menus can be a little intimidating at first glance. In addition to crime fiction, the Tangled Web also offers a limited amount of information on fantasy, science fiction, horror and audiobooks.

A site for crime aficionados who want to be kept up to date on their favourite authors, new crime novels and prize winners.

http://home.vicnet.net.au/~ozlit/		
Ozlit		
Overall rating: ★ ★ ★		
Classification: Directory	**Readability:**	★ ★ ★
Updating: Unclear	**Content:**	★ ★ ★ ★
Navigation: ★ ★ ★ ★	**Speed:**	★ ★ ★ ★
AU		

Ozlit houses a multitude of links to websites primarily concerned with Australian writing, including magazines, publishers and writers' organisations, together with a database of information on Australian authors. As the welcome message on the homepage suggests, the site requires patience to fully explore but the OzLit Lists and the Authors Lists provide two easy routes in. Other parts of the site deal with poetry, children's literature and research, which offers links to a miscellany of discussion groups, catalogues and libraries. The use of frames makes the site reasonably easy to navigate although, inevitably, they restrict your view of its contents. Updating seems to be sporadic, with many things labelled as new which are not, a subject of some complaint in the Messages/Guest Book area. Inevitably, with such a vast number of links, some are broken but despite these criticisms, OzLit remains a tremendous resource to readers, students and writers of Australian literature.

OzLit's ambitious directory of Australian literary sites sometimes overreaches itself but there is still much of value to explore.

reference

Whether you need a thesaurus or an encyclopedia, Bible search facilities or a rhyming dictionary, you should find many of the reference tools you need on the internet. Some sites do use reference texts that are out of copyright, so if you're looking for bang up to date information, it's probably best to use a publisher's site such as Oxford University Press's Ask Oxford. Most sites are still accessible for free. Britannica.com, the Encyclopedia Britannica's unrivalled reference website, charges a subscription fee but for such a magnificent source of information on just about everything under the sun, this seems a small price to pay.

www.askoxford.com			
Ask Oxford			
Overall rating: ★ ★ ★ ★ ★			
Classification:	Information	**Readability:**	★ ★ ★ ★
Updating:	Daily	**Content:**	★ ★ ★ ★ ★
Navigation:	★ ★ ★ ★ ★	**Speed:**	★ ★ ★ ★
(UK)			

The Oxford University Press's reference website offers the opportunity to search their Dictionary, Thesaurus, Dictionary of Quotations and Dictionary of First Names, along with expert advice on writing and solving gritty grammar problems. The homepage's Word of the Day and Quote of the Week will please trivia addicts, who should also find plenty to occupy them in the Games pages. The site is easy to navigate with a search box to the top right of the screen and a pushbutton bar across the top, plus links to other OUP sites.

SPECIAL FEATURES

Ask the Experts leads to a set of Collective Terms plus Jargon Buster, which demystifies grammatical terms. The Oxford Word and Language Service FAQs page aims to answer many common queries but also offers the opportunity to email them if you're still flummoxed.

Better Writing offers expert advice on writing reports, essays and dissertations and writing for the internet, all taken from books published on the subject. This section also includes advice on plain English and how to avoid common linguistic errors as well as a page on emails and text messaging.

This site puts OUP's unrivalled expertise in English language reference publishing at your fingertips.

www.britannica.com

Britannica.com

Overall rating: ★ ★ ★			
Classification: Information		**Readability:**	★ ★ ★
Updating: Daily		**Content:**	★ ★ ★ ★ ★
Navigation: ★ ★ ★		**Speed:**	★ ★ ★

US 🔒

Free access to one of the internet's finest sources of information on everything under the sun always seemed a bit too good to be true and Britannica.com now charges a subscription which can be paid either monthly or annually. There is a free trial period, although you will have to remember to cancel the subscription after the first fourteen days. The homepage gives a flavour of what's on offer with links to today's news at the *New York Times*, pointers to the kind of articles to be found at the site, and descriptions of browsing options. Searches can be confined to the Encyclopedia, websites, Merriam's Collegiate dictionary and thesaurus, or extended to the entire site. Search results indicate which entries are available only to subscribers, although non-subscribers can read the first few paragraphs, and include links to relevant websites and magazine articles outside the Britannica site. Britannica's own entries are authoritative; in-depth articles and links outside the site are wide-ranging. Navigation can be a little rudimentary in places and you will need to use your browser Back button. Speed can also be an issue but these are small criticisms considering the unrivalled extent and quality of knowledge and expertise offered at this site. The separate Britannica School site is aimed largely at American teachers and students, although some of its features, such as self-study courses in basic computer skills and access to all three of Britannica's encyclopedias, will be of interest to all.

SPECIAL FEATURES

Britannica's Heritage is an archive of articles commissioned from key figures for the Encyclopedia, ranging from Sigmund Freud writing on the development of psychoanalysis, to Harry Houdini on conjuring. The heritage archive can be reached from the bottom of the homepage.

Britannica's World Atlas can be browsed by country and covers all aspects, from climate to history, with suggestions for further reading.

Year in Review Going back to 1997, this facility consolidates information for a particular year, from significant dates to events in all areas, from fashion to science.

Well worth the subscription, Britannica.com offers authoritative information on just about everything under the sun.

www.peevish.co.uk/slang
A Dictionary of Slang

Overall rating: ★ ★ ★ ★ ★			
Classification:	Information	Readability:	★ ★ ★ ★
Updating:	Monthly	Content:	★ ★ ★ ★ ★
Navigation:	★ ★ ★ ★ ★	Speed:	★ ★ ★ ★

(UK)

From abdabs to zonked, this simple site is a dictionary of British slang which can either be searched or browsed. Definitions provide the approximate period of origin, country of derivation if outside the UK, and examples to clarify where necessary. The introductory essay examines the way in which slang adapts itself, often passing from sub-cultures into everyday language, and includes a nicely worded apology about the possible offensiveness of some expressions included in the dictionary, with an explanation as to why they are there. The News section currently contains links to a few articles on slang, alongside other news about the site and Bibliography offers a list of recommended reading. Readers are invited to submit entries for inclusion but are asked to read the introductory essay first.

SPECIAL FEATURES

Links is an extensive list covering sites dealing with many categories of slang including Australian, Crime and Prison Slang and Gay/Lesbian Slang, to name but a few.

An excellent resource for tracking down definitions for even the most colourful British slang.

www.yourdictionary.com
Your Dictionary .

Overall rating: ★ ★ ★ ★ ★			
Classification:	Information	Readability:	★ ★ ★ ★
Updating:	Regularly	Content:	★ ★ ★ ★ ★
Navigation:	★ ★ ★ ★	Speed:	★ ★ ★ ★

(US)

If you find yourself continuing to read the dictionary after looking up a word, be prepared to spend a lot of time at this one-stop language reference site. Its many features include speciality dictionaries, grammars, language dictionaries, a thesaurus and a straightforward English dictionary, as well as language identifiers, links to language research papers, ranging from Latin grammar to a comparison of Estonian and Finnish, and a collection of entries in the Library section which includes the world's longest word and an essay on the possibility of chimpanzees learning to talk. The English dictionary and thesaurus are based on the Merriam Webster Collegiate editions and are comparatively easy to use with a help page which clearly explains the lengthy definitions. In the unlikely event that none of the links at the site leads to a suitable dictionary for your needs, click the Other Indexes button for a list of other online language sites. There's a word of the day for those wishing to expand their vocabulary and you can register to receive it by email. Easy to navigate, with all functions accessible either from the buttons at the bottom of the page or from the homepage, this site is rich in content for anyone fascinated by language while providing a simple reference tool for those who need it.

SPECIAL FEATURES

Speciality Dictionaries range from accounting to sailing.

Language Dictionaries contains over 250 languages and can be a bit intimidating with a large number of entries for each language, including speciality dictionaries. In addition to the dictionaries, a fee-paying translation service has recently been introduced at the site. For those interested in different languages, the Endangered Language Repository has a set of entries devoted to languages which are in danger of fading out of use.

The Game Room will please word game fans with crosswords of all kinds available in a variety of languages, and a long list of links to sites, ranging from online vocabulary quizzes to the Klingon Language Institute. Those who enjoy a laugh at the expense of academics should visit the Postmodernist Scholarship Generator from the YDC Non-Writing Center box.

A treasure box of information for those fascinated by language, this site can also be used as a simple reference tool.

OTHER SITES OF INTEREST

The Bible Gateway
http://bible.gospelcom.net

This web page offers search facilities for a variety of versions of the Bible, from the traditional King James to the New International Version. Searches can be made either by passage or by key words. If you find yourself mystified by the abbreviations listed in the drop-down menu accompanying both search boxes, click on Advanced Search which reveals which abbreviation refers to which version of the Bible to be searched.

Rhyme Zone
www.rhymezone.com

This rhyming dictionary site offers synonyms, antonyms, related words and definitions in addition to rhymes. The results of searches are reasonably comprehensive although care needs to be taken with spelling as this is an American site. The texts of both the Old and New Testaments can be accessed from here and the complete works of Shakespeare can be searched by phrase to track down a particular quotation. It's also possible to search a dictionary of quotations which includes quotes from Laurie Anderson to Victor Hugo.

Annabelle's Quotation Guide
http://annabelle.net

This site may be a little too pink for some people's tastes but both its subject and its author search results outstrip many other more complicated quotation sites on the internet. Once you've found the appropriate quotation you can send it to a friend via a QuoteGram.

Webnexus: Desk References page
www.ntworld.org/webnexus/page10.html

This Desk Reference page of the theological site, WebNexus, offers a gateway to many reference sites other than those concerned with religion, although if you're looking for an Ugaritic grammar, this is the place to come. Split into three areas, Atlases, Dictionaries, Grammars & Translators, and Encyclopaedias, the page has links to a wide variety of sites including a Roman atlas, Latin dictionaries and grammars, a Catholic Encyclopaedia and the Internet Encyclopaedia of Philosophy. Well worth a visit for the curious.

literature published on the web

For book lovers, one of the great bonuses of the internet is free online access to books that are now out of copyright. Listed below you'll find several sites which offer an easy route into an enormous range of books and journal archives. You'll also find sites which showcase new writing and offer the chance for you to voice your opinions. And for those of you who have wholly embraced the electronic age and have discovered the joys of downloading e-books, you'll find several sites offering books by new writers you won't find in high street bookshops alongside bestsellers.

http://digital.library.upenn.edu/books
The Online Books Page Books Listings

Overall rating: ★ ★ ★ ★ ★			
Classification:	Directory	Readability:	★ ★ ★ ★
Updating:	Regularly	Content:	★ ★ ★ ★ ★
Navigation:	★ ★ ★ ★ ★	Speed:	★ ★ ★ ★ ★

US

Hosted by the University of Pennsylvania Library, this web page offers a straightforward route to over 14,000 texts, now out of copyright, published online. In addition to a search facility by author or title, the site's listings can be browsed by subject. Click on Serials to browse a directory of journals and magazines. News of what's happening, both at this site and in the world of online texts, can be accessed from the homepage, while the Inside Story offers a set of FAQs.

SPECIAL FEATURES

Features currently highlights three particular areas with a link to the Celebration of Women Writers sister site, an essay on banned books online, which includes links to the relevant texts, and an index to prize winning texts available online.

Archives includes a set of links to sites which house specialist or foreign language texts.

News includes well-organised lists of new additions to the site, arranged in date order.

This simple, efficient directory is an invaluable tool for navigating the multitude of texts available online.

www.poets-corner.com
The Poet's Corner

Overall rating: ★ ★ ★ ★ ★			
Classification:	Enthusiasts	Readability:	★ ★ ★ ★
Updating:	Regularly	Content:	★ ★ ★ ★ ★
Navigation:	★ ★ ★ ★ ★	Speed:	★ ★ ★ ★ ★

US

This is a site put together by enthusiasts for enthusiasts and it certainly hits the spot. It currently includes over 6,000 poems and is updated on a regular, almost daily, basis. The site is easy to navigate using the bar to the left of the screen, but it's worth reading the introductory essay on the homepage to gain a flavour of the care that has gone in to creating this site, as well as what it has to offer. It includes not only poetry, but also a set of brief biographical notes on a small selection of poets, a portrait gallery and a set of recommended anthologies, major works and collections. The site was founded in 1994 by Steve Spanoudis whose enthusiasm for the internet is as passionate as his love of poetry, if the list of sites he maintains, found under Home, is anything to go by.

SPECIAL FEATURES

Daily Poetry Break is chosen by Bob Blair who provides a commentary on the poem which may include biographical or historical details or Bob's reflections on the poem.

Subject Index is a novel way to search the poetry database. Click on a subject, from Animals to Weather, to find a set of poems that fit your chosen theme.

Favourites Each of the site's four editors has selected his favourite poems and explained the reasons for choosing them.

Mutual Links includes links to a variety of poetry and quotations sites but is well worth visiting for the richly eclectic mix of links to other sites from a Thomas the Tank Engine page to an Alfred Hitchcock site.

Other Works is worth visiting for a list of poems recommended by the editors, which can't be added to the site for copyright reasons.

An excellent site for poetry lovers with a pleasingly idiosyncratic feel.

www.promo.net/pg/
Project Gutenberg

Overall rating: ★ ★ ★ ★ ★			
Classification:	Directory	**Readability:**	★ ★ ★ ★
Updating:	Regularly	**Content:**	★ ★ ★ ★ ★
Navigation:	★ ★ ★ ★ ★	**Speed:**	★ ★ ★ ★ ★

US

Set up in 1971, Project Gutenberg's mission is to provide free online access to as many classic literary texts as possible. If you want to learn about the background to the project, the left-hand menu offers articles, past newsletters and a detailed essay on its origins. A visit to What books will I find in Project Gutenberg, part of the FAQs page, explains the situation on copyright. Don't be put off by the occasionally intimidating technical references to FTP files and the like, the site is simple to use and texts can be browsed by author or title. Books can either be downloaded as text or in the speedier zipped file format. For the latter, you will need either WinZip or PKZip software to unzip the files. Access to all texts is free but donations are welcome.

This pioneering site offers a route into a rich selection of classic literature for free.

www.all-story.com/index.cgi

Zoetrope: All-Story

Overall rating: ★ ★ ★ ★ ★

Classification:	Magazine	**Readability:**	★ ★ ★ ★
Updating:	Monthly	**Content:**	★ ★ ★ ★ ★
Navigation:	★ ★ ★ ★	**Speed:**	★ ★ ★ ★

US

This is a great site for short story enthusiasts. Part of Francis Coppola's website, Zoetrope: All-Story is a monthly magazine featuring short stories and the occasional essay or one-act play. Writers range from Graham Greene and William Faulkner to Rick Moody and Melissa Bank. Back issues are available and information about the authors can be reached by clicking on their name at the top of the story. Some stories listed are only available in the print edition of the magazine. Writers can submit their own work through the Virtual Studio. Registration with the studio is free and members receive feedback on their work. The site also runs creative writing workshops online.

SPECIAL FEATURE

Live Story reached through Events, Live Story offers a selection of short story readings. The stories take some time to download so it's worth waiting a few minutes before following the instructions to reinstall Windows MediaPlayer which appear under Note.

A real treat for short story readers.

www.onlineoriginals.com

Online Originals

Overall rating: ★ ★ ★ ★

Classification:	Ecommerce	**Readability:**	★ ★ ★
Updating:	Unclear	**Content:**	★ ★ ★ ★ ★
Navigation:	★ ★ ★	**Speed:**	★ ★ ★ ★

UK

Established in 1996, Online Orginals are pioneers of e-book publishing in the UK. As the name suggests, Online Originals' e-books are only available from this site. The company has gained something of a reputation for its critical expertise, as a visit to their media coverage page, reached through About, will show. For those unfamiliar with e-books, the FAQ section contains a straightforward, jargon-free guide on what you receive when you buy an e-book and the various means of reading it. The catalogues are easy to browse both by subject and by the four available e-book formats, Palm, PC or Mac, Pocket PC or Printable. Book synopses are brief, but samples can be read online and a click on the author's name will display a short biography. Submissions for publication are invited.

SPECIAL FEATURES

Visually Impaired people are specially catered for by Online Originals who have produced three e-books, compatible with speech synthesis and Braille software.

Francais offers a small selection of e-books in French.

The UK's pioneering e-book publisher's site.

OTHER SITES OF INTEREST

BookSelecta
www.bookselecta.com
Bookselecta offers free downloads of books by unpublished authors alongside a selection of classic texts. Registration is required to download a book and you will need Microsoft Reader, available via a link from Bookselecta, to read it. The site has been set up to provide a platform for writers trying to get their work published and readers are warned that many of the manuscripts are unedited. A free writers' pack is available for those who want to submit their work. The bookshop sells a wide range of e-books by established authors with discounts on offer for those who choose to pay an annual fee for membership of the Readers' Club.

Bartleby.com: Great Books Online
www.bartleby.com/
Bartleby's Great Books Online provides a gateway to a wide selection of online texts ranging from poetry to Gray's Anatomy. The homepage offers a variety of methods for searching the database, including browsing verse, fiction, non-fiction and reference, together with author, subject and title indexes. A further set of indexes to particular texts, such as the King James Bible, the World Factbook and the Oxford Shakespeare, is also available. Texts are clearly displayed, chapter by chapter, with an option to search by key words. The homepage also features a daily dip into the texts with a poem, a quotation, a biography and a definition.

The Complete Works of Shakepeare
http://the-tech.mit.edu/Shakespeare/works.html
Although there's no sign of this site being completely restored to its former glory after a catastrophic disk failure, it's still the simplest way to access Shakespeare's plays online. The plays can either be read scene by scene or the complete text can be displayed on one page.

The Internet Public Library Online Texts Collection
www.ipl.org/reading/books
Part of the School of Information at the University of Michigan, the Internet Public Library's Online Texts Collection web page offers a gateway to over 17,000 online texts available. Searches can be made alphabetically by author or title, by category, using the Dewey classification system, or by using key words. New entries can be listed by title or author.

for writers

developing skills and getting published

If you want to develop your writing skills but don't have the time or the resources to enrol in a full time course, you may find that the internet provides the answer. As well as online writing courses, you'll also find opportunities to get published and a supportive community in which to exchange views and information, and get constructive feedback on your work. Courses are usually designed to be taken at your own pace, so that they can be fitted into a busy life, and you may well find yourself corresponding with fellow writers from all over the world.

www.getoutthere.bt.com/index2.cfm

Get Out There

Overall rating: ★ ★ ★ ★ ★

Classification:	Magazine	Readability:	★ ★ ★
Updating:	Monthly	Content:	★ ★ ★ ★ ★
Navigation:	★ ★ ★	Speed:	★ ★ ★

UK R

Set up by British Telecom to help people trying to break in to the highly competitive fields of music, film, photography and writing, the Get Out There site is an excellent source of practical advice and encouragement, providing a supportive community and forum for discussion. To get the best out of the site, you will need to register as a member which allows you to join discussions, enter competitions and upload your work for others to read. The main homepage is split into four, offering a taster of what's available with a feature for each of the disciplines and links to Editor's Choice at the bottom of the page. Before visiting the Writing area, it's worth exploring the Info section, accessible from the top left of the screen, which explains the philosophy behind the site and what it has to offer.

Click on the Writing button at the top of the screen to display a navigation bar which opens up the site to you. The homepage highlights the site's latest features plus news of competitions and uploads of new writing. Choose Editorial from the navigation bar for features on new writers in Breaking Talent, profiles of established writers and editors in Spotlight On, lots of sound advice in How To and a collection of miscellaneous articles on writing in Talking Head. Run your mouse along the Editorial navigation bar to extend it and find Minute Dispute, short debates on genres and other aspects of writing. Click on Library from the main Writing navigation bar for the opportunity to read work that has been uploaded to the site and offer your comments. The Tools option from the Writing bar offers software which allows you to create a collection of work from Get Out There to download and read offline.

You will need to select the Community pushbutton from the top of the screen to get involved in discussions, checkout the classifieds or enter a chat room. Discussions are friendly and supportive with lots of regular contributors. Use the Zone box to the left of the screen to restrict content to the writing area of the site. The drop-down Category menu can be used to refine listings further.

This site offers a host of useful features for aspiring writers and it takes time to fully explore all that it has to offer. Navigation can sometimes be a little tricky and, if you're not used to frames, you may find the restricted view a little frustrating but that said, Get Out There provides an invaluable resource for any one who is serious about breaking into writing.

SPECIAL FEATURES

How To is a collection of articles in the Editorial section which concentrate on the nitty-gritty of writing, offering sound, practical advice on topics such as putting together a book proposal or breaking into travel writing.

Library is a collection of work uploaded by members. Work can be added via the Upload function on the Writing navigation bar and members can also add their comments on writing already in the Library, using the Review button. Comments are constructive and supportive, often resulting in exchanges between author and reviewer.

Competitions are built around various forms of writing and offer the chance to win free books as well as having your work read and assessed by objective and knowledgeable judges. Get Out There has strong links with top literary agent Curtis Brown, and with the publisher, HarperCollins

Classifieds are well worth exploring for opportunities to sell your work. Use the Zone or Category boxes to the left of the screen to restrict the listing to your area of expertise.

Links offer a wider range of links to useful sites from writers' magazines to market sites seeking work from writers.

Downloads describes software tools for writing and editing and offers links to sites from which they can be downloaded.

Discussions range across a variety of topics and can be searched via the drop-down menu to the left. Exchanges are friendly and supportive.

This excellent site offers support, practical advice and a strong sense of community for writers who are serious about getting their work published.

OTHER SITES OF INTEREST

ABCtales
www.abctales.com
Set up by John Bird, founder of *The Big Issue*, ABCtales encourages writers to submit stories for publication at the site which currently hosts well over 7,000 stories and poems, ranging from 50 to 2000 words. The handy cherry-picked symbol alerts readers to the pick of the crop but you'll need to register to read anything rated PG. Writers who want to submit their work need to register and can choose the level of privacy they want as well as whether they want readers to rate their work. There's a lively discussion board and the site's homepage changes daily. A well-organised set of links leads to many sites for both writers and readers. Check out Freebies for writing competitions plus links to other competition sites.

Online Originals
www.onlineoriginals.com
As part of its pioneering role as a publisher of original work in e-book form, Online Originals invites writers to submit work for publication at their site. All writers must submit their work for review by a published Online Original author but prospective writers can choose who they would like to review their work. Visit Submissions for author biographies, together with samples of the author's work, to help you pick a reviewer. It's worth bearing in mind that you will have to pay a fee to have your work reviewed but you will receive critical feedback together with a score from 1 to 10. If two reviewers rate the manuscript as 9 or 10, a contract is issued to the submitter. Details of royalties paid to authors published by Online Originals can be found in FAQs.

Write 4 Kids

www.write4kids.com/

Some UK writers may find the relentlessly bright tone of this American site a little trying but it is worth exploring for its Articles and Tips page which offers advice to those just starting out. The site is highly commercial with lots of encouragement to sign up for its monthly Children's Book Insider newsletter, together with articles promoting books published by Laura Backes, who runs the site, but there is enough to explore for free to decide whether this is the site for you or not.

Zoetrope: All-Story

www.all-story.com/index.cgi

Part of Francis Coppola's Zoetrope site, Zoetrope: All-Story offers online writing courses for short story writers and also invites submissions for publication. Registration with the studio is free and members receive constructive feedback on their work. Visit the Writing Workshops area of the site for the Online Class Tour which offers sample reading lists and course materials together with a set of FAQs and detailed outlines of how the courses work.

resources

These sites offer sound advice on the practicalities of writing, from preparing a manuscript for publication to copyright law, plus community, support and market information. Many of the sites have been put together by writers who are both familiar with the difficulties of starting out and well acquainted with the perennial bugbears of the writing life such as isolation and insecurity. Their aim is to offer a network of resources together with the chance to get in touch with other writers and be kept up to date with information about your own area of interest.

www.burryman.com			
The Burry Man Writers Centre			
Overall rating: ★ ★ ★ ★ ★			
Classification: Resources		**Readability:**	★ ★ ★
Updating: Daily		**Content:**	★ ★ ★ ★ ★
Navigation: ★ ★ ★ ★ ★		**Speed:**	★ ★ ★ ★
US			

Although this is primarily a writers' resources site there's enough content here, including the list of entertaining websites in Diversions and the page devoted to Scotland, to capture the interest of the casual visitor. All that's available at the site is listed on the menu to the left of the homepage but the help page, found via the hyperlink at the top of the screen, neatly summarises the contents of each section. Links to recommended websites together with relevant books, which can be bought via a direct link to either amazon.com or amazon.co.uk, appear to the right of all pages. There are resource pages for Fiction Writing, Health Writing, History & Sciences, Science Fiction & Horror, Screenwriting and Stage & Radio, together with links for freelance writers. A regular email newsletter keeps you up to date with additions to the site and there's encouragement to share your successes by emailing them to the Burry Man. Although most of the sites listed are American, many UK sites are also included along with several Australian and Canadian links. The international appeal of the site is clear from the country listing at the bottom of the Writing Centres page. An excellent resource for writers, this is a simple site to find your way around although the green text on black background can be a bit of a strain after a while. And in case you're wondering, the Burry Man is a figure from Scottish folklore who walks the streets of the small fishing village of South Queensferry, near Edinburgh, on the second Friday in August exchanging good luck for whisky and cash.

SPECIAL FEATURES

Articles for Writers written by Joseph Hayes, who co-runs the site, these articles offer sound, no-nonsense and often inspiring advice on topics such as getting published, setting up your own website, and dealing with those dreaded rejection slips.

Diversions Inject some fun into the serious business of writing with some great displacement activities offered by this list of sites including Africam, which transmits live pictures from African game reserves, the Chocolate Lovers' Page and the Lego website. You can always call it research.

Scotland The Burry Man is co-run by Scottish-born Jennifer Greenhill-Taylor and devised by Walter Wood, a Scottish architect, hence this section devoted to all things Scottish. As well as webcam sites trained on various areas of Scotland, including Loch Ness, this section includes links to a long list of newspapers and magazines plus sites devoted to Scottish history and all aspects of Scottish life from cookery to sport.

Research should save a great deal of time for writers trying to get their facts right. Categorised into sections such as Libraries, Find an Expert, and Art and Images, this section offers access to a wide variety of reference websites.

Screenwriting and Stage & Radio These particularly extensive resource indexes also includes a long list of links for drama writers.

Writing Centres includes retreats, writing courses and arts organisations from around the world.

An excellent writers' resource site with enough unusual content to interest the casual visitor.

www.scalar.com/mw/
misc.Writing

Overall rating: ★ ★ ★ ★

Classification:	Reference	**Readability:**	★ ★ ★ ★
Updating:	Regularly	**Content:**	★ ★ ★ ★ ★
Navigation:	★ ★ ★ ★ ★	**Speed:**	★ ★ ★ ★

CA

Packed with useful information for both professional writers and novices, this website has an invaluable set of links to information and resources. In addition to acting as an index, the homepage lists the current writing site of the week, homepages for newsgroup members, the misc.Writing Charter plus a lengthy set of Posting Guidelines for the newsgroup. The Writers' Marketplace section has links to articles on marketing work while Writing Basics includes features on how to build yourself a daily routine plus salient tips on research, writing fiction and some basic style guides. Although the site is based in Canada much of the information here is applicable in the UK.

SPECIAL FEATURES

Starting Point can be used as a basic toolkit by new writers and includes a list of writers' organisations in Australia, New Zealand, Canada, the United Kingdom and the USA.

FAQ offers advice on an extensive list of topics ranging from preparing a manuscript to listings of writers' newsgroups.

Sound practical advice plus a handy reference point make this an invaluable resource for new writers.

www.wordpool.co.uk/wfc/wfc.htm
The Wordpool

Overall rating: ★ ★ ★ ★

Classification:	Information	**Readability:**	★ ★ ★ ★
Updating:	Regularly	**Content:**	★ ★ ★ ★ ★
Navigation:	★ ★ ★ ★ ★	**Speed:**	★ ★ ★ ★

UK

Part of the Wordpool site devoted to children's books, the Writing for Children section is an excellent source of advice and support for children's writers and those trying to get published. Written by Diane Kimpton, an established children's writer, the site contains articles on practicalities such as book-keeping and computer skills together with features on how to set about finding a publisher and what kind of book is required for the Literacy Hour. There is also a discussion list and a diary of events aimed specifically at children's writers. A set of useful links and a page devoted to children's book news rounds off this well-thought out resource nicely.

An excellent site for children's writers, both new and established.

www.author-network.com

Author Network.com

Overall rating: ★ ★ ★			
Classification:	Information	**Readability:**	★ ★ ★ ★
Updating:	Regularly	**Content:**	★ ★ ★ ★ ★
Navigation:	★ ★ ★	**Speed:**	★ ★ ★ ★

UK

The homepage of this writers' resource site is so crammed with information that first-time visitors may feel a little intimidated but its worth taking the time to browse it as if it were a newspaper's front page. Divided in to three sections, the middle section of the page highlights some of the features at the site plus news such as prize announcements and may include work opportunities together with contact details. The right-hand section lists some of the site's articles, ranging from tips on publicising your work to writing guides, and may include advance information of writing competitions. The left-hand section acts as the site's menu with a list of resource links by genre, plus general resources, including recommendations of books for writers, a critique service, creative writing courses and information on copyright. Once away from the homepage, the menu becomes slightly abbreviated. On a first visit it's worth using the drop-down menu at the top of the subsidiary pages to visit Using This Site so that you can get an idea of which parts best suit your needs. Feedback about the site is actively encouraged and although sadly underused, the message board is worth checking out for notices flagging up publishers seeking submissions. There is much of value for both professional writers and those trying to get published in any field, ranging from screenwriters to poets, but it takes some time to get to grips with all that's on offer here.

SPECIAL FEATURES

Puff Adder Books   The Writers Network enthusiastically promotes e-books and publishes its own list through Puff Adder Books, reached from left of the homepage. Submissions are welcome and there is a comprehensive set of guidelines detailing requirements together with a sample contract. E-books are in PDF format and can be bought securely at the site with sample chapters to download for free.

Links by Genre   appears on the left-hand menu of the homepage. Each genre heading leads to a page of carefully selected links for sites ranging from resources, organisations, markets and magazines dedicated to a variety of genres, ranging from horror writing to travel.

Small Presses   is an annotated list of magazines who are receptive to work from new writers.

Content Sites   reached describes a small set of websites which offer an opportunity to be published online.

UK Literary Agents   is a list of agents which indicates areas of interest and includes contact details.

A useful resource site for both professional writers and those wanting to find a way of breaking into publishing, this site can appear a little overwhelming at first but a little effort repays dividends.

www.writers.net
Writers Net

Overall rating: ★ ★ ★ ★			
Classification:	Information	**Readability:**	★ ★ ★ ★
Updating:	Daily	**Content:**	★ ★ ★ ★
Navigation:	★ ★ ★ ★	**Speed:**	★ ★ ★ ★

(US)

Writers Net is split into four areas covering writers, agents, editors and publishers, each of whom has their own page and listings directory, although the publishers section of the site is still being developed. In addition to the directories, the site aims to bring all sections of the writing/publishing world together in a range of forums which offer a chance to exchange views and ask questions. It also includes articles covering practical issues such as setting about finding a literary agent, both in the US and the UK, and a set of links to other useful research and resource sites.

SPECIAL FEATURES

Discussion   All forums seem to be reasonably well-frequented but the agents' and writers' forums are by far the most popular. Contributors bounce ideas off each other, ask for tips and air their anxieties, most of which meet with a friendly and helpful response. Lots of regular contributors help to give the discussion boards a community feel.

Although predominantly visited by writers, this site aims to bring together all aspects of the writing/publishing business in a number of discussion forums.

OTHER SITES OF INTEREST

Bloomsbury Magazine: Writers' Area
www.bloomsburymagazine.com
Click on the Writers' Area icon on Bloomsbury Publishing's homepage to find their Guide for Unpublished Writers which offers nitty-gritty practical advice on getting published. The Law section lists books which deal with thorny issues such as libel and copyright while the Calendar section has details of awards, festivals and literary competitions with contact information available if you click on the name. Extracts from *The Writers' and Artists' Yearbook* offer advice on approaching publishers and submitting material. Advice from an established literary agent is backed up with a list of agents, both in the UK and Ireland, and in the United States. The Web Directory offers a long list of links to organisations, from arts councils to writers' associations.

Writers-circles.com
www.writers-circles.com/
Run by the author of the *UK Directory of Writer's Circles*, this site is a handy resource directory for UK writers which includes links to a small selection of writing circles. Other resources include links to reference tools, genre sites, writers' organisations and magazines for writers. The Competitions section lists writing competitions complete with contact details. There's also a diary of events and listings for literature festivals plus a message board for writers hoping to make contact with each other.

The Writers' Guild of Great Britain
www.writersguild.org.uk

Set up in 1958, the Writers' Guild of Great Britain aims to protect writers' interests by keeping them informed on issues such as intellectual property rights, and negotiating minimum terms agreements with a variety of bodies, from publishers to the BBC. The Guild's website has information on payment in the Rates and Issues section, while pages on writing for film, radio, theatre, books, and TV offer short news items. It's worth checking Facts and Opinions for a first-person account of working in the field. The Links and Misc section has links to a variety of useful organisations, from newspapers to trade associations. A full listing of member benefits plus details of how to join can be found in the About Us section.

miscellany

literary Prizes

---

www.bookerprize.co.uk
The Man Booker Prize

★★★★★

This site is at its busiest from the announcement of the Man Booker Prize shortlist in mid-September, to mid-October, when the winner of the UK's best-known literary prize finally learns their fate. The result is posted at the site shortly after its announcement at the televised awards dinner. In between times, a brief history of the prize, a flavour of the reactions of previous winners together with any news, such as the announcement of the current year's judges, can be found here. Readers can also vote for their favourite nominee, as soon as the shortlist is announced. Previous winners together with shortlists and judges can all be traced back to the first Booker prize, awarded in 1969. This is a slightly cumbersome two-step operation in order that the book jacket may be displayed but it can be bypassed by clicking on the View by Author and Book Title option, although the list will be displayed in alphabetical, rather than chronological, order.

www.commonwealthwriters.com
Commonwealth Writers Prize

★★★★★

This attractive website showcases winners of the Best Book and Best First Book prizes, for books written in English by Commonwealth authors. Past winners include Peter Carey, Louis de Bernières and Vikram Seth. The homepage features the current winners, both overall and regional. Judges' comments, author biographies and press releases can also be accessed. The site is easily navigable using the links to the left of the screen and includes details of past winners.

www.impacdublinaward.ie
The International IMPAC Dublin Literary Award

★★★★★

First awarded in 1996, the IMPAC award is one of the most prestigious international literary awards with its prize of IR£100,000. The current winner is featured on the IMPAC website's homepage with a link to News where the complete shortlist can be found, together with links to reviews, and authors' homepages, if available. The Award Archive, accessible from the top of the homepage, can be searched by year for details of past winners which include a biographical sketch of the author and a synopsis of the winning novel, together with links to both the shortlist and a complete list of nominations. FAQs supplies a full history of the prize and its nomination rules.

http://www.nobel.se
The Nobel Prize

★★★★★

This site houses details of all Nobel Laureates, starting in 1901 when the prize was established. The homepage features details of the current Laureates for each Nobel category, together with recent articles about winners, past and present. For details of past Laureates, click on the subject of your choice displayed at the top of the screen. A complete record is kept for each Laureate including the presentation speech, a biography page complete with full bibliography, extracts from the winning book (for literature Laureates), and videos of the presentation and lecture, where they exist. The latter require RealPlayer software. Full details about the history of the prize, including its founder Alfred Nobel, can be found by clicking Nobel on the subject bar.

www.orangeprize.co.uk
The Orange Prize for Fiction

★★★

Set up in 1996, the Orange Prize for Fiction has fast become one of the most talked about literary prizes in the UK, with its aim to promote and celebrate novels written by women. Part of the Orange telecomm site, these pages showcase both the current winner and the remaining five shortlisted books, with extracts, reviews and biographies for each nominee. Use the links under Prize for Fiction to the right of the screen to find out the latest news and events connected to the prize, read details of past winners, the current shortlist and longlist, plus thumbnail sketches of the judges. Response can be a little slow.

www.pulitzer.org//index.html
The Pulitzer Prizes

★★★★

One of America's most prestigious arts awards, the Pulitzer Prizes have been running since 1917. Details of winners for a particular year can be found by clicking the appropriate year on the timeline at the top of the screen. Journalism, for which the award was first created, appears at the top with Letters, Drama and Music mid-way down the page. Click on the Archive link to search for brief biographies of award winners, the full text of their award-wining article, the award citation and the names of the jurors. The site also features a biography of Joseph Pulitzer, together with a history of the prizes set up to commemorate one of the America's finest journalists. Other interesting nuggets of Pulitzer information can be found in the FAQ part of the site.

www.whitbread-bookawards.co.uk
Whitbread Book Awards

★★★

Details of the current Whitbread Book of the Year and Whitbread Children's Book of the Year remain on the Latest News page of this site, along with other announcements such as who will be on each judging panel, until the new round of announcements in January. Listings of winners together with the First Novel, Biography, Poetry and Novel awards can be found in the Past winners section, although only details of title, author and publisher are available.

literature festivals

www.britishcouncil.org/arts/literature/festivals
British Council – UK Literature Festivals

★★★★★

This literature festival listings site can be searched by region, month or name of the festival. The regional option offers a map as well as a set of geographical areas to choose from. Festival entries include contact details and links to websites where appropriate, together with dates and a brief description of the festival programme. Although some organisations seem to be better at providing information than others, this simple site is a useful reference point for those who enjoy the blossoming UK festival scene.

www.cheltenhamfestivals.co.uk
Cheltenham Festivals

★★★★

This is the umbrella site for Cheltenham's many festivals which range from jazz to literature. The literature festival is usually held during October and details of events are posted around August. Click on your chosen festival at the top of the screen to display a set of labelled pushbuttons. These lead to details of other events, such as the literature festival's new spring weekend break and Write Away courses, as well as information about the main festival. A useful link to Cheltenham's tourist information website can be found by clicking Venues at the top right of the screen. There's the chance to request a brochure or give feedback via the Ask a Question box to the left of the screen. Online bookings can be made by email.

www.edbookfest.co.uk
Edinburgh International Book Festival

★★★

This site lists full details of events at Edinburgh's lively August literature festival, including its separate children's programme. The programme can be searched by key words to track down your favourite author. You'll need Flash software to view this site, but it's easily downloadable, free of charge, via the link on the welcome page.

www.hayfestival.co.uk
Hay Festival

★★★★★

If it's too early to find out about what's going on at the UK's best-known literature festival, the last one can be revisited at this friendly, well-organised website. Details of the last festival's programme, an archive of audio files and an email diary will all give a flavour of what's in store for those who have never visited this marathon literary event. There are links to tourist information sites for accommodation details and travel information plus the opportunity to sign up for news bulletins about Hay. The new festival programme is added to the site around February or March.

other sites

www.ask-a-librarian.org.uk
Ask a Librarian

Overall rating: ★ ★ ★ ★ ★			
Classification: Information		**Readability:**	★ ★ ★ ★ ★
Updating: Unclear		**Content:**	★ ★ ★ ★ ★
Navigation: ★ ★ ★ ★ ★		**Speed:**	★ ★ ★ ★ ★

UK

This simple but brilliant little site offers the opportunity to put a factual question to a librarian. Questions are fed into a network of public libraries in the UK. A set of clear instructions on how to ask your question is displayed ahead of the question form and it's essential to read this to get the best out of the site. This facility is aimed mainly at UK residents, and although questions from other parts of the world have been answered, a set of appropriate links is provided for non-UK visitors. A visit to the Some Questions and Answers part of the site is a treat for those with a taste for trivia.

SPECIAL FEATURES

Participating Libraries takes you to a set of direct links to public library websites. More useful links can be found on the Tips on Asking Your Question page including one to The Public Records Office.

An excellent resource for asking questions on a multitude of topics from books to sport.

www.poems.com
Poetry Daily

Overall rating: ★ ★ ★ ★			
Classification:	Enthusiast	**Readability:**	★ ★ ★ ★
Updating:	Dating	**Content:**	★ ★ ★ ★ ★
Navigation:	★ ★ ★ ★	**Speed:**	★ ★ ★ ★

US

www.bookbrowse.com
BookBrowse.com

Overall rating: ★ ★ ★			
Classification:	Enthusiast	**Readability:**	★ ★ ★ ★
Updating:	Weekly	**Content:**	★ ★ ★ ★ ★
Navigation:	★ ★ ★ ★ ★	**Speed:**	★ ★ ★ ★ ★

US

Fans of contemporary poetry might find themselves tempted to make this attractive site their homepage. Each day a new poem is featured at the site, together with details of the poet's background. The poem is chosen to reflect some aspect of the date, whether it be topical or seasonal. The site's layout is simple and it can be easily navigated from the links at the bottom of the screen, but a visit to About PD, with its thoughtful welcoming letter complete with several appropriate poems, is a pleasant way to become acquainted with its contents. You will also be invited to register for a free weekly newsletter.

SPECIAL FEATURES

Archive can be browsed by poet, date or title. Past Features are often interesting and inventive, and there is also a small collection of interviews with contemporary American poets.

News provides a set of links to news articles about poetry plus a list of new books. Click on the title to be taken to amazon.com for a review and the opportunity to buy the book.

An attractive showcase for contemporary American poetry.

Bookbrowse.com's slogan, 'don't judge a book by its cover, read it for yourself at BookBrowse.com' sums up what's available at this privately run site. A growing bank of book extracts supplemented by press reviews, author interviews and in some cases, reading group guides, covers a range of books by popular literary authors, from Jane Hamilton and Alice Hoffman to Nick Hornby and Harold Bloom. The aim of the site's owners is to provide enough material to make an informed choice about what you want to read next. The horizontal navigation bars at the top and bottom of the screen offer browsing by author, title and category as well as interviews, bestseller lists and reading group guides. New entries are highlighted on the homepage and there is an opportunity to browse both recent and future publications. A link to book trade news headlines can also be found under Key Links.

An excellent independent site where you can read book extracts before making your next reading choice.

www.bookcrossing.com
Book Crossing

Overall rating: ★ ★ ★ ★			
Classification:	Enthusiast	**Readability:**	★ ★ ★ ★
Updating:	Daily	**Content:**	★ ★ ★ ★
Navigation:	★ ★ ★ ★ ★	**Speed:**	★ ★ ★ ★ ★

US

Set up by IT executive Ron Hornbaker as a community project, this site is an imaginative extension of the reading group idea and now has participating members across the world from the United States to Malaysia. The concept is simple and the process easy, as long as you can bear to part with your books. If you have enjoyed a particular book and want to share it with others, take up free membership of the Book Crossing club, print off a Book Crossing label, attach it to your book and release it 'into the wild' by registering it at Book Crossing then leaving it in a public place. You can track the progress of your book through Book Crossing's website and you can also 'go hunting' for books in the wild by searching for recently released books in your country.

SPECIAL FEATURES

The Forum   Reached via Community, the Forum hosts discussions in Spanish, Italian and German as well as lively exchanges in English.

This site offers a novel way of exchanging both books and ideas with other readers.

www.whichbook.net
Whichbook.net

Overall rating: ★ ★ ★ ★			
Classification:	Information	**Readability:**	★ ★ ★ ★
Updating:	Unclear	**Content:**	★ ★ ★ ★
Navigation:	★ ★ ★ ★	**Speed:**	★ ★ ★ ★ ★

UK

Whichbook.net offers a novel way to choose fiction and poetry to suit your mood or taste. There's a helpful tutorial which tells you how to indicate whether you want something happy or sad, easy or demanding, conventional or weird. You can choose up to four of the 12 criteria on offer and there's further scope for pinpointing your choice in the box beneath, which offers the chance to specify plot, character or setting. Whichbook.net searches its database for books which match your choices and displays the results, together with a brief synopsis and further suggestions. Books are graded as Best match, Good match or Fair match and in the main, results are remarkably apt. Some book extracts can be read online. Searches can also be confined to audiobooks or large print books.

SPECIAL FEATURES

Borrow   Click the Borrow button to check if the selected book is available from your local library.

For those who can't decide what to read, this site offers a novel solution by matching mood and taste to its extensive database of book titles.

OTHER SITES OF INTEREST

Book-a-Minute
http://www.rinkworks.com/bookaminute/
Not enough time to read books? This site just might be the answer. Rinkworks have condensed hundreds of books, from *Huckleberry Finn* to *2001: A Space Odyssey* into handy one-minute summaries with often hilarious results. The site is divided in to Bedtime, for children, Classics, and Science Fiction/Fantasy. Readers are invited to vote for the next condensed book. Definitely worth bookmarking for a quick burst of humour on a dull day as is the equally funny sister site, Movie-a-Minute.

BookBrowser
www.bookbrowser.com
Set up by a librarian from Indiana in 1996, BookBrowser has now joined with Barnes and Noble. It offers a collection of book reviews and recommendations based around three basic categories of reading lists, broken down by sub-genre. If, for instance, you would like to see all detective stories set in the Renaissance, you can browse the Time Periods section of the Mystery and Crime reading list. Most books on the lists have reviews that briefly outline the plot and offer a critical summary. Reviews can also be browsed by genre, ranging from Detective/Mystery to Western. All editions referred to at the site are American although many of the books reviewed are also published in the UK.

The British Library
www.bl.uk
This website acts as a window into the British Library offering overviews of its extensive collections which includes the National Sound Archive. The drop-down menu on the homepage can be used to find out what you can see without visiting the library and what to expect if you do. Several of the library's treasures may be viewed online including the Gutenberg Bible and a translation of the Magna Carta. Background information on projects such as the electronic Beowulf (now available on CD-Rom) can also be accessed. A visit to the Site Map gives a useful overview of what's available at this well-organised and extensive site.

If You Like This...
http://library.christchurch.org.nz/Guides/IfYouLike/
The principle of this clever web page is simple. Click on a category that appeals, ranging from John Grisham to Cult Fiction, Crime Novels That Walk on the Wild Side to *Angela's Ashes*, and a page of suggested authors will be displayed. The homepage is split into Fiction, Detective and Mystery Fiction, Biographies, New Zealand Fiction and Contemporary Women Writers, although the latter only appears as a link at the top of the screen. The site also includes a small music section towards the bottom. Part of New Zealand's Christchurch City Libraries' website, this is the next best thing to asking a librarian or bookseller for recommendations.

Word of Mouth
www.word-of-mouth.org.uk
Set up by Opening the Book, the same organisation who run Whichbook.net (see left) this site also aims to recommend books to readers in search of something new. Click on Buzz, Challenge or Indulgence for recommendations that fit the bill. Comments about the books are contributed by readers

registered at the site together with their reasons for choosing them plus a list of other books they've enjoyed. Those who choose to register set up a profile for themselves based on a set of multiple choice questions at registration. Free registration entitles members to suggest books, match their profile against other members to find books that they might like to read and join in discussions at the forum.

Index

2001: A Space Odyssey 138
ABCtales 125
About.com: Women Writers 53
academic books 19, 20, 46, 108, 109
  see also, educational books
Achebe, Chinua 54, 73
Achuka 82
Ackroyd, Peter 51
Adbooks 83
Adrian Mole's Diary 76
Advanced Book Exchange 29
advice, see new writers
African American Review, the 50
Age, the 80
Alcott, Louisa May 75
Al Fayed, Mohamed 76
Alibris 30
Almond, David 92
amazon.com 13, 36, 39, 49, 83, 104,
  126, 136
amazon.co.uk 12, 16, 39, 49, 71, 76,
  80, 82, 86, 87, 93, 100, 126
American Authors on the Web 53
American literature 53, 108, 126, 128
American National Biography Online,
  the 60
American Rivers Authority, the 14
Amis, Martin 36
Ancient and Medieval History Book
  Club, the 33
Anderson, Laurie 116
Andromeda 27
Angela's Ashes, Frank McCourt 138
Angelou, Maya 65
Animal Dreams, Barbara Kingsolver
  42
Annabelle's Quotation Guide 116
Anniinina's Toni Morrison Page 50
anthologies 94, 119
anthropology 60
antiquarian books 29-31
  see also, rare books
architecture 20, 21, 64
Ariel, Sylvia Plath 101, 104
Armitage, Simon 109
Arnott, Jake 64
art 20, 21, 25, 33, 58, 64, 93, 108, 127
Arts & Letters Daily 69

Arts-books.com 21
Arts Guild, the 32, 33
Ask a Librarian 135
Ask Oxford 113
Asterix, Goscinny and Uderzo 93
Atlantic Monthly, the 74
Atlantic Online, the 74
Atlantic Unbound 75
atlases 114, 117
Atwood, Margaret 15, 36
Auden, W. H. 78
audio books 21, 72, 79, 89, 112, 137
Auel, Jean 64
Austen, Jane 36, 37, 53
Austen.com 37
Auster, Paul 100, 104
Australian, the 69
Australian literature 17, 69, 73, 80, 111,
  112, 126, 128
Author Network.com 129
authors 15, 16, 35-54, 107, 110, 129
  interviews 12-14, 16-18, 32-34, 36,
  42, 45, 48, 49, 56, 58, 61, 64-67,
  71-75, 78-80, 82, 91, 92, 98, 100-105,
  110, 112, 136
  see also, biography, new writers
Authors Discussed in the Victorian
  Web 53
aviation 28, 33
awards, see grants, literary prizes

Babysitters Club 92
Backes, Laura 126
backlist books 23, 58, 121
Bacon, Francis 47
Ballard, J. G. 74
ballet 21, 71
Bank, Melissa 121
Banks, Iain M. 51, 64, 71
banned books online 119
Barbara Kingsolver 42
Barefoot Books 89
bargain books, see book clubs,
  discounted books
Barnes & Noble.com 15, 71, 138
Barrett, Andrea 105
Bartleby.com: Great Books Online 122
Bastulli Mystery Library 52

BBC, the 51, 131
BBC Book Club Online 100
BBC Books 53, 73
Bear, Greg 64
Beckett, Samuel 43
Bedford/St Martins 108
Bellow, Saul 74
Bellwether Prize, the 42
Beowulf 138
bereavement, see children's issues as
  subjects for fiction
bestsellers 17, 32, 42, 78, 104
  children's 85
  lists 12, 13, 16, 18, 65, 66
Bible, the 47, 57, 108, 116, 122, 138
Bible Gateway, the 116
bibliographies 39, 50, 52, 82, 108, 115,
  134
  see also, reading lists
Big Issue, the 125
Big Sleep, the, Raymond Chandler 38
biographies 19, 21, 24, 27, 50, 60,
  102, 104, 107, 122, 134, 138
  of authors and poets 32, 34, 36-47,
  50-54, 61-64, 70, 73, 76, 98, 102, 104,
  105, 108, 119, 121, 124, 132, 133, 136
Black studies 108
Blackwell's 19
Blake, Quentin 90
blind people 34, 121
Bloom, Harold 136
Bloomsbury 56
  Authors 54
  Magazine: Bloomsbury Reading Club
  105
  Magazine: Writers' Area 130
Blue Coupe 70
BMJ Bookshop 26
Bol.com 34
book2book 67, 71
Book-a-Minute 138
bookbinders 31
BookBrowse.com 136
BookBrowser 138
Bookcase 53
Book Club, Radio 4 100
book clubs 15, 31-34
Book Crossing 137

Bookends 16
Booker Prize 133
Book Fairs, Scholastic 92
Book Hive, the 88
Booklover, the 18
Book People, the 17
Book Place, the 16
Books at Transworld 65
  Reading Guides 105
Books Direct 31
BookSelecta 122
Bookseller, the 65
bookselling trade, the 65-67, 136
Books for Children 32
Books for Cooks 22
bookshops 66
Books Sales Yearbook, the 65
Bookstart 84, 111
Booktrust 84, 111
Booktrusted.com 84
Book Week, Children's 84
Bookwire 67
Boston Globe 69
Boswell, James 50
Bourdain, Anthony 76
Braille 121
Bridget Jones, Helen Fielding 32
Britannica.com 114
British Council – UK Literature Festivals
  134
British Dyslexia Organisation, the 85
British Library, the 139
British Telecom 124
Brodsky, Joseph 63
Brontë Parsonage Museum 37
Brontë Society, the 37
Brooks, Terry 64
Browning, Elizabeth Barrett 111
Bryson, Bill 65
Buffy the Vampire Slayer 16
bullying, see children's issues as
  subjects for fiction
Bunker, Eddie 71
Burgess, Melvin 83, 98
Burns, Robert 50
Burroughs, William S. 74
Burry Man Writers Centre, the 126
Business and Finance Bookshop 22

Bussell, Darcey 71

Canadian literature 53, 126, 128
Canongate Books 57
Canterbury Tales, the, Geoffrey Chaucer 39
Carcanet 63
careers in the bookselling trade 66, 129
Carey, Peter 132
Carnegie Library, the 50
Carnegie Medal, the 82
Carpet People, the, Terry Pratchett 46
Carr, Caleb 80
Carter, Angela 102
Catherton.com 52
Celyn Jones, Russell 71
Chandler, Raymond 38
Channel 4 Books 64
Charles Dickens Page, the 39
Chaucer, Geoffrey 39
Cheltenham Festivals 134
children's;
  books 14, 19, 32, 34, 56, 58, 59, 60, 62, 64, 67, 73, 79, 81-98, 111, 112, 126, 128, 133, 134, 138
  issues as subjects for fiction 83, 85, 87, 91
  see also, reading difficulties
Children's Literature Web Guide, the 88
Classic and Sports Car 28
classics, the 47, 84, 88, 108, 120, 122, 138
climbing 28
clubs, see book clubs
Cole, Babette 83
collectors, see rare books
Collins, Wilkie 53
Colour of Magic, the, Terry Pratchett 46
Commonwealth Writers Prize 132
competitions for new writers 125, 129, 130
Complete Works of Shakespeare, the 122
Computer Manuals Online Bookstore 22
Conan Doyle, Sir Arthur 40
conservation of books 30, 31
Contemporary literature 109, 138
Cooke, Alistair 69
cookery 22, 32, 53, 62, 64, 70, 127
Cool-reads 85

copyright 107, 111, 119, 120, 126, 129, 130
Country Bookshop 16
courses 15, 56, 110, 121, 126, 127, 129
  see also, new writers
Cowley, Jason 16
Crime and Punishment, Fyodor Dostoyevsky 100
Crime Time 71, 80
crime writing 23, 38, 52, 70, 71, 73, 80, 112, 138
critical theory 108
critics, see reviews
cult fiction 54, 138
currency converter 29
Curtis Brown 125

Dahl, Roald 94
Dante 111
David, Elizabeth 62
Davis, Lindsey 62
Dawkins, Richard 51
Deary, Terry 95
Deaver, Jeffery 52
de Bernières, Louis 57, 102, 132
Demon Dog Central 71
Derbyshire Writers' Guild, the 37
design 21, 33, 64
detective books, see crime writing
developing skills as a writer, see new writers
Dibdin, Michael 80
Dickens, Charles 39
dictionaries 24, 60, 92, 107, 113-117
Dictionary of Slang, a 115
Diedrick, James 36
difficulties, see children's issues as subjects for fiction, reading difficulties
digital libraries 30
Dilbert 70
discounted books 15, 17, 20, 22, 34, 59, 65, 101, 102, 105, 122
  see also, book clubs
Discworld 45, 46, 87
Diski, Jenny 105
Divine Secrets of the Ya-Ya Sisterhood, Rebecca Wells 104
diving 28
divorce, see children's issues as subjects for fiction
Doctor Seuss 96
Donne, John 47
Dorling Kindersley 58
Dostoyevsky, Fyodor 100

drama 23, 108, 121, 122, 126, 127, 131, 133
Duffy, Carol Ann 109
Dunmore, Helen 105
Dymocks Booksellers 17
dyslexia 85
dyspraxia 87

Eastern European literature 111
e-books 15, 17, 20, 43, 45, 59, 62, 67, 107, 119-122, 125
Eco, Umberto 43
Economist, the 69
Eden Project, the 65
Edinburgh International Book Festival, the 57, 134
educational books 17, 82, 87, 91, 92, 95, 109, 110
  see also, academic books, children's books
eighteenth-century literature 108
Element 58
Eliot, T. S. 77
Ellroy, James 71, 80
Elmer, David McKee 90
e-mail updates;
  new publications 12, 13, 19, 26, 59, 77, 82, 104
  searches for books 23, 29, 31
encyclopaedias 114, 117
English language teaching 60, 91, 113
Escape 33
essays 36-38, 41, 42, 45, 54, 69, 71, 73, 75, 76, 80, 98, 108, 115, 119, 121
evolution 26
excerpts, see extracts
exchange of books 137
exhibitions, art 33
Expert Gardener series 65
extracts 12, 13, 16, 17, 32, 34, 56, 58, 62-65, 70, 92, 101-105, 121, 133, 136, 138
  read by authors and poets 49, 72, 73, 78
ezines 68-74, 110

Faludi, Susan 104
Family History Books 25
fan sites, see authors
fantasy, see science fiction, fantasy and horror
Fantasy and SF Book Club 32
fashion 21
Faulkner, William 121

Faulks, Sebastian 62
feminism, see women's studies and literature
festivals 57, 134, 135
Fforde, Jasper 40
Fforde Grand Central 40
fiction 19, 21, 24, 25, 27, 33, 62, 70, 75, 108, 122, 126, 128, 133, 134, 138
  see also, authors, children's books, crime, cult fiction, romance, science fiction, fantasy and horror, reading groups, short stories, women's studies and literature, etc.
Fielding, Helen 32, 104
film 21, 23, 24, 126, 127, 129, 131
Fine, Anne 84
Finnegan's Wake, James Joyce 41
Fireandwater.com: Authors 54
  see also, HarperCollins
first editions 29, 31
  see also, rare books
Fischer, Tibor 71
Fisk, Robert 69
food, see cookery
foreign language books, dictionaries and discussion 24, 116, 119, 121, 137
Fourth Estate 63
Foyles 17
Franzen, John 72
Freud, Sigmund 114

Gabriel Garcia Marquez 43
Gale, Patrick 79
galleries, art 33
gambling 24
games 40, 46, 48, 64, 93, 95, 96, 113, 116
  see also, computer
Garcia Marquez, Gabriel 43, 104
Garden Books by Post 24
gardening 24, 65
gay and lesbian 25
Gay's the Word 25
genealogy 25, 107
Geoffreychaucer.org 39
George Orwell 1903-50, the 45
Get Out There 124
getting published, see new writers
Gibson, William 74
gifts, see merchandise
Globe Theatre, the 47
Good Book Guide, the 34
Goosebumps 92
grammar 113, 115-117

Granta 64
Grant and Cutler 24
grants for writers 111
Graves, Robert 63
Gray's Anatomy 122
Greene, Graham 121
Grisham, John 139
Guardian, the 49, 51, 65, 76, 100
Guardian Unlimited;
  Books 76
  Reading Group 100
  The Authors 51
guides for reading groups 103, 104
Gunroom, the 44
Gutenberg Bible, the 138

Hammett, Dashiell 101
Hammicks 16
  Legal Bookshops 26
Hamilton, Jane 72, 136
Hardy, Thomas 41
HarperCollins 54, 63, 125
  Fire and Water 58
  Reading Guides 104
Harris, Joanne 65, 105
Harry Potter series, J. K. Rowling 16, 56, 76, 96
Hay-on-Wye literary festival 36, 135
health 126
  see also, medical, mind, body and spirit, self-help
Heaney, Seamus 77
Hellenga, Robert 104
Hemingway, Ernest 72
Hergé Foundation, the 97
High Stakes 24
High Window, the, Raymond Chandler 38
Hildebrandt, Greg and Tim 48
Hinton, S. E. 84
His Dark Materials trilogy, Philip Pullman 98
history 21, 25, 27, 28, 33, 44, 47, 58, 92, 94, 95, 104, 114, 117, 126, 127
  see also, romance
History Bookshop.com 25
History Guild, the 33
Hitchcock, Alfred 120
Hodder Headline 64
Hoffman, Alice 137
Holden, Wendy 64
home-based book selling business 93
Home Software World Club 32

Hornby, Nick 51, 62, 137
Horrible Histories, Geography, etc. 92, 95
horror, see science fiction, fantasy and horror
Houdini, Harry 114
Howe, John 48
Huckleberry Finn, Mark Twain 138
Hughes, Frieda 51
Hughes, Ted 51, 73
Hugo, Victor 116
humanities 60
Hypnerotomachia Poliphili 65

If You Like This ... 138
IMPAC award, the 132
improving written English 113
Independent, the 79
Indian literature 111
In Harry's Bar in Venice, Ernest Hemingway 72
intellectual property rights 131
  see also, copyright
International IMPAC Dublin Literary Award, the 132
Internet Bookshop, the 17
Internet Encyclopedia of Philosophy, the 117
Internet Public Library Online Texts Collection, the 122
Internet Theatre Bookshop, the 23
interviews, see authors
Interzone 110
Irish literature 108
irvinewelsh.com 49
Irvine Welsh Hole, the 49
Irving, John 32, 50
issues, see children's

Jacket 73
Jacques, Brian 97
Jakubowski, Maxim 23
January Magazine 70
Jarman, Derek 74
Jeanette Winterson: The Official Site 49
Jerusalem Post, the 69
Jewish literature 108
John Irving is God 50
Johnson, Samuel 50
Jordan, Robert 64
journalism 45, 49, 69, 75, 133
  see also, newspapers

journals 119
  see also, magazines
Joyce, James 41

Kafka 52
kamera.co.uk 71
Katie Morag series, Mairi Hedderwick 90
Keillor, Garrison 72
Kennedy, A. L. 74
Keyes, Marian 32
Kids at Random House 90
Killing the Buddha 69
King, Stephen 42
Kingsolver, Barbara 42, 103
Kneale, Matthew 79

Lamb, Charles and Mary 47
languages, see foreign language
large print books 138
Latin American literature 43, 56
Latino literature 108
laureates, Nobel 133
law 26, 60
Lawson, Nigella 32
Leaves of Grass, Walt Whitman 75
lectures 36, 39
lesbian 25
letters 134
libraries 30, 31, 50, 66, 107, 109, 112, 119, 122, 135, 137, 138
lists, see bestsellers, reading lists
Literacy Hour, the 87, 128
literary;
  agents 66, 125, 129, 130
  prizes 14, 42, 43, 57, 82, 85, 107, 111, 112, 119, 129, 130, 132-134
  resources 107-112
  see also, reference books
Literary Resources on the Net 108
literature festivals 57, 134, 135
Litlinks 108
Litt, Toby 101
Little, Brown 64
Lively, Penelope 34
local history 25
London Review of Books, the 76, 80
London's Talking Bookshop 21
Lonely Planet 59
Lord of the Rings, J. R. R. Tolkien 48
L-Space Web, the 45, 46

Macmillan Children's 64

magazines 74-80, 119, 129
  see also, ezines and individual magazines listed
Magical Realism 43, 56
Magma 21
Mail on Sunday, the 102
Maltese Falcon, the, Dashiell Hammett 101
Man Booker Prize, the 133
Mango 32
Mansell, Jill 32
Mansfield Park, Jane Austen 37
manufacturing 22
maps 19, 28
Margaret Atwood Reference Site 36
maritime 25, 28, 44
Martin Amis Web, the 36
Master and Commander, Patrick O'Brian 44
maths, difficulties in learning 87
McClaren, Malcolm 76
McCourt, Frank 104, 138
McEwan, Ian 102
McInerney, Jay 78
medical 26, 60
medieval studies and literature 39, 47, 109
Melvin Burgess Homepage 98
merchandise 16, 27, 38, 48, 97, 98
Merriam Webster Collegiate dictionary and thesaurus 114, 115
military 25, 28, 33
Military and Aviation Book Society, the 33
Mill, John Stuart 53
mime 21
mind, body and spirit 58, 62
Mitchell, Chris 74
Modern World 43
Moody, Rick 72, 121
Morpurgo, Michael 83
Morrison, Toni 50
Motion, Andrew 34
Motor Books 28
Motorsport and Classic Cars 28
multimedia, see computer
Murder One 23
music 26, 60, 63, 93, 133
Music Books r Us 26
Mystery and Thriller Club, the 32
  see also, crime writing

Nabokov, Vladimir 36, 75

Nasmith, Ted 48
Native American literature 108
National Library for the Blind, the 34
National Poetry Competition, the 109
National Poetry Day 109
Natural History Bookshop 26
nautical, see maritime
New Scientist 69
newspapers 74-80
  see also, individual newspapers
  listed
New Statesman, the 16
new writers 15, 111, 121, 124-131, 134
New Yorker, the 49, 69
New York Times, the 50, 65, 77, 114
New Zealand literature 111, 128, 138
Nobel Prize, the 43, 133
non-fiction 82, 104, 122
  see also, reference books
Noon, Jeff 74
novels, see authors, fiction
nuclear engineering 22

O'Brian, Patrick 44
Obscure Store 70
Observer, the 76
O'Faolain, Julia 71
Official Asterix Website, the 93
Official Robert Burns Site, the 50
Oliver, Jamie 32
Onion 70
online books, see e-books
Online Books Page Books Listings, the
  119
Online Originals 121, 125
Opening the Book 138
Oprah's Book Club 103
Orange Prize for Fiction, the 133
Orbit Books 64
Ordnance Survey, the 19
Orwell, George 45, 51
Ottakar's 15, 16
out-of-print titles 23, 26, 29-31
Owlswick Press 27
Oxford English Dictionary 60
Oxford Literacy Web, the 92
Oxford Maths Zone, the 92
Oxford University Press 60, 113, 122
  Children's and Reference 92
  Word and Language Service 113
Ozlit 112

palaeontology 26
Palmquist, Mike 109

Pan Macmillan 64
parenting 58, 84, 87
Patrick O'Brian Page, the 44
Paulsen, Gary 84
Payback Press 57
payment for writers 131
Penguin 61
  Classics 61
  Putnam 104
  Readers Group 101
Perfect Storm 104
performing arts, see drama
Pet Book Shop 27
Peter Rabbit Official Website, the 98
philosophy 108, 117
photography 21, 33
Picador 64
Picard, Liza 34
picture books 82, 92
  see also, children's books
plain English 113
Plath, Sylvia 51, 78, 101, 104
Plathonline.com 51
Plato 108
plays, see drama
pmpoetry 111
poetry 14, 36, 38, 41, 42, 45, 50, 51,
  53, 54, 56, 60, 62, 63, 71, 73, 75, 78,
  101, 104, 108-112, 116, 119, 122, 125,
  129, 134, 136
  children's 82, 85, 88, 92
Poetry and Writers Magazine 14
Poetry Daily 137
Poetry News 109
Poetry Review 109
Poetry Society, the 85, 109
Poet's Corner 119
Poisonwood Bible, Barbara Kingsolver
  103
Politico's Bookstore 27
politics 27
postmodernism 36
Potter, Beatrix 98
Powell's City of Books 14
Pratchett, Terry 45, 46, 65, 87, 110
price checking 18, 107
  see also, discounted books
prizes, see literary prizes
Profbooks.com 22
profiles, see authors' interviews,
  biography
Project Gutenberg 120
Prospect 69
Proulx, Annie 64, 108

Public Records Office, the 135
publishers, see bookselling trade and
  individual publishers listed
Publishers Weekly 67
Publishing News 16, 66
Puff Adder Books 129
Puffin 91
Pulitzer Prizes, the 133
Pullman, Philip 79, 92, 98
Pynchon, Thomas 43

QPD 32
questions for discussion, see reading
  groups
quotations 116, 120, 122
  see also, extracts

Radio 4 *Book Club* 100
radio writing 126, 127, 131
Railway Club, the 33
Random House 62, 90, 96
  Readers Group 102
Rankin, Ian 112
rare books 14, 19, 20, 27, 29-31
Raymond Chandler Website, the 38
Reader, the, Bernard Schlink 103
reading;
  difficulties 83, 85, 87
  groups 42, 44, 56, 61, 62, 64, 65, 76,
  100-105, 107, 111, 112, 136, 137
  lists 12, 19, 36, 82, 86, 87, 107, 108,
  110, 138
Reading Group Guides.com 103
Reading Matters 86
recommendations 12-14, 16, 18, 32,
  44, 56, 58, 61, 63, 64, 78, 102, 105,
  107, 119, 120, 129, 137, 138
  by authors and poets 34, 36, 49, 70,
  72, 76-79, 101, 110,
  children's 82-91
  see also, reading groups
recruitment, see careers
Red House, the 34
Redwall Abbey 97
reference books 24, 56, 58, 60, 92,
  107, 112-117, 122
Regency on the Web, the 37
religions 116
  see also, Bible, the
Rendell, Ruth 52
research 112, 127, 128
  see also, literary resources, reference
  books
resources, see literary resources

Resources for Booksellers and Book
  Collectors 31
reviews 12-15, 19-21, 23, 25-28, 32-
  34, 36, 49, 51, 58, 69-80, 100-104,
  107, 110, 121, 125, 129, 133, 136, 138
  children's 82-88
Rhyme Zone 116
RIBA Bookshop 20
Richmond Review, the 71
Rinkworks 139
Roald Dahl Fans.com 94
Roald Dahl Official Site 94
Robinson, Kim Stanley 110
romance 23, 33, 52, 73, 107
Rough Guides 63
Rowling, J. K. 54, 92, 96
  see also, *Harry Potter*
Rushdie, Salman 71
Russell, Willy 105

Salon 51, 69
Salon.com 72
Samson, Polly 65
Samuel French 23
Samuel Johnson Sound Bite Page, the
  50
Sassoon, Siegfried 109
Schama, Simon 16
Schlink, Bernard 103
Scholastic 92
schools, see educational books
science 26, 58, 60, 93, 126
science fiction, fantasy and horror 15,
  23, 27, 32, 52, 53, 59, 64, 73, 98, 107,
  110, 112, 126, 129, 138
Scotland 127
screenplays, see film
second-hand books 14, 20, 23, 24, 27,
  29-31, 137
Self, Will 54, 57, 74
self-help 53
selling books as a home-based
  business 93
Seth, Vikram 133
Seussville 96
SF Site, the 110
Shakespeare, William 46, 47, 116, 122
Sherlock Holmes 40
Sherlockian.net 40
Shields, Carol 54, 64
Shields, Jody 105
Shipleys 20
Shivers, Terry Deary 95
short stories 71, 75, 94, 121, 125, 126

Shreve, Anita 105
signed editions 27, 28, 31, 58, 90
Silver Moon bookshop, the 17
Simon and Schuster 104
Skating to Antarctica, Jenny Diski 105
Slater, Nigel 64
Smith, Zadie 32
Sobel, Dava 64
South African literature 111
specialist bookshops 19-28
speech synthesis 121
Spenser, Edmund 47
Spike magazine 49, 71, 74
Spiral-Bound newsletter 43
sport 28, 87, 93, 127
Sports Books Direct 28
stage writing, see drama
Stanfords 28
starting out as a writer, see new writers
Stephen King Website 42
Stiffed, Susan Faludi 104
students, see academic books, reading lists
suggested reading, see recommendations
Sunday Times, the 79
Swindells, Robert 92
Swotbooks.com 20

Tales from Shakespeare, Charles and Mary Lamb 47
Talking Bookshop, the 21
Tangled Web UK 112
Taste 32
teachers, see academic books, educational books
teaching English as a foreign language, see English language teaching
technical 14
teenage writing 82, 83, 98, 107
Telegraph, the 69, 79
television 21, 131
Terry Deary 95
Thames & Hudson 64
theatre, see drama
Theatre of Cruelty, Terry Pratchett 45
thesauri 113-115
Thomas Hardy's World 41
Thomas the Tank Engine, the Rev. W. Awdry 120
Thorsons 58

thrillers, see mystery
Thursday Next 40
Timbuktu, Paul Auster 100
Time magazine 73
Times, the 49
Times Literary Supplement, the 77
time travel 84
Time Warner 105
Tintin.com 97
Tolkien, J. R. R. 16, 48
Tonkin, Boyd 79
training, see courses
translators 117
transport 28
Transworld 65
Tranter, John 73
Trapido, Barbara 79
travel 21, 28, 58-60, 63, 105, 124, 129
Tremain, Rose 104
Trollope, Joanna 54, 73
true crime, see crime
True Mysteries, Terry Deary
TSP 32
twentieth-century literature 108
Tyler, Anne 62, 102
typography 21

UK Directory of Writers' Circles, the 130
University of Michigan 122
University of Pennsylvania Library, the 119
unpublished writers, see new writers
Updike, John 75
Usborne Publishing 93

veterinary science 22
Victorian Britain 39, 40, 53
Victorian Web 53
Vine, Barbara 52
Virago 65
Virgil 39
visually-impaired people, reading aids for 121
Voyage of the Narwhal, the, Andrea Barrett 105

Waterstone's 16
Webnexus: Desk References page 116
Weir, Alison 32
Wells, Rebecca 104
Welsh, Irvine 49, 74
Whichbook.net 137, 138
Whitbread Book Awards 134

White, Antonia 65
Whitman, Walt 75
W H Smith 17, 46
Williams, Tad 64
Wilson, A. N. 79
Wilson, Jacqueline 90, 92
Wilson-Okamura, David 39
Winfrey, Oprah 103
Winnie the Pooh 98
Winterson, Jeanette 49
Wolfe, Tom 15, 70
Women's Review of Books, the 65
women's studies and literature 17, 53, 65, 73, 76, 108, 119, 133, 138
Word of Mouth 139
Word Pool, the 87, 128
Wordsworth, William 53
Work in Progress 41
World Book Dealers 30
World Books 32
World of Art 64
Write 4 Kids 126
Writers' and Artists' Yearbook, the 130
Writers-circles.com 130
Writers' Guild of Great Britain, the 131
Writers Net 130
writing, see new writers, research
written English, advice on improving 113
W. W. Norton 44
Yahoo Clubs: Reading Groups 103
Yahoo News: Harry Potter Page 96
Yellow Admiral, the, Patrick O'Brian 44
young adults, see teenage writing
Your Dictionary 115
You Reading Group 102
Zephaniah, Benjamin 73
Zoetrope: All-Story 121, 126
Zola, Emile 51